First World War

and Army of Occupation

War Diary

France, Belgium and Germany

41 DIVISION
Divisional Troops
Divisional Trench Mortar Batteries
17 May 1916 - 29 October 1917

WO95/2625/5

The Naval & Military Press Ltd
www.nmarchive.com
Published in association with The National Archives

Published by

The Naval & Military Press Ltd

Unit 10 Ridgewood Industrial Park,

Uckfield, East Sussex,

TN22 5QE England

Tel: +44 (0) 1825 749494

www.naval-military-press.com

www.nmarchive.com

This diary has been reprinted in facsimile from the original. Any imperfections are inevitably reproduced and the quality may fall short of modern type and cartographic standards.

Contents

Document type	Place/Title	Date From	Date To
Heading	41st Division Trench Mortar Batts. May 1916-Oct 1917 Mar 1918-Oct 1918 Italy 1917 Nov-1918 Feb		
Heading	WO95/2625/7 41 Div Div Trench Mortar Battery May 1916-Oct 1917		
War Diary	Sheet 38 B. 23 d 48	17/05/1916	26/05/1916
War Diary		25/05/1916	31/05/1916
Miscellaneous	D.A.G., 3rd. Echelon Base.	04/07/1917	04/07/1917
War Diary		02/06/1916	30/06/1916
War Diary	Sheet 28 S.W	08/06/1916	08/06/1916
War Diary	U.27 d 9.9.	08/06/1916	08/06/1916
War Diary	U.27.b.9.6	08/06/1916	08/06/1916
War Diary	C.4.a. 1/2.6.	30/06/1916	30/06/1916
War Diary	U.27 d 9.9	30/06/1916	30/06/1916
War Diary	U.27 b.9.6	30/06/1916	30/06/1916
War Diary	U.15 c 5 1/2.9	30/06/1916	30/06/1916
War Diary	U.15.d.0.4 1/2	30/06/1916	30/06/1916
War Diary	Sheet 28 S.W.	30/06/1916	30/06/1916
War Diary	U 27 d 9.9	08/06/1916	08/06/1916
War Diary	U 27 b 9.6.	08/06/1916	08/06/1916
War Diary	C 4 a 1/2.6	30/06/1916	30/06/1916
War Diary	U 27.d 9.9	30/06/1916	30/06/1916
War Diary	U.27 b 9.6.	30/06/1916	30/06/1916
War Diary	U 15 c 5 1/2.9.	30/06/1916	30/06/1916
War Diary	U 15 d 0. 4 1/2	30/06/1916	30/06/1916
War Diary	Sheet 28 S.W.	04/07/1916	04/07/1916
War Diary	U.15.d.0.4 1/2	04/07/1916	04/07/1916
War Diary	U 15 d 1.5 1/2	08/07/1916	08/07/1916
Miscellaneous	U.14.b	10/07/1916	10/07/1916
War Diary	U.15 d.0.4 1/2	10/07/1916	12/07/1916
War Diary	U.15 d 0.4 1/2	12/07/1916	12/07/1916
War Diary	U.15 d 1.5 1/2	14/07/1916	14/07/1916
War Diary	U.27.6 8 1/2	16/07/1916	16/07/1916
War Diary	U 15 d 1.5 1/2	16/07/1916	16/07/1916
War Diary	Sheet 36 N.W.	16/07/1916	24/07/1916
War Diary	C 4 C.7.7 1/4	24/07/1916	24/07/1916
War Diary	Sheet 28. S.W.	24/07/1916	24/07/1916
War Diary	U 27 b 8 1/2	24/07/1916	24/07/1916
War Diary	U 21.a 7.7.	24/07/1916	24/07/1916
War Diary	U 15 d 1.5 1/2	25/07/1916	25/07/1916
War Diary	Sheet 28. S.W.	25/07/1916	25/07/1916
War Diary	U 27 b.8 1/2 1.	25/07/1916	25/07/1916
War Diary	U 21 a 7.7	25/07/1916	25/07/1916
War Diary	Sheet 36 N.W.	26/07/1916	26/07/1916
War Diary	C 4 C 7.7 1/4	26/07/1916	26/07/1916
War Diary	Sheet 28. S.W U 27 b 8 1/2	26/07/1916	26/07/1916
War Diary	U 21 a 7.7	26/07/1916	26/07/1916
War Diary	Sheet 28 S.W	07/08/1916	08/08/1916
War Diary	41st Div Front	23/08/1916	23/08/1916
War Diary	Epagne	01/09/1916	01/09/1916
War Diary	Ailly	02/09/1916	02/09/1916

War Diary	Dernancourt	10/09/1916	30/09/1916
War Diary	Epagne	01/09/1916	01/09/1916
War Diary	Ailly	02/09/1916	02/09/1916
War Diary	Albert	10/09/1916	12/09/1916
War Diary	W of Delville	12/09/1916	12/09/1916
War Diary	Wood Sheet 78	13/09/1916	14/09/1916
War Diary	Mametz	17/09/1916	19/09/1916
War Diary	S 22 b 7.9.	24/09/1916	28/09/1916
War Diary	Mametz	17/09/1916	24/09/1916
War Diary	W of Delville	24/09/1916	30/09/1916
War Diary	Epagne	01/09/1916	01/09/1916
War Diary	Ailly	02/09/1916	02/09/1916
War Diary	Dernacourt	03/09/1916	10/09/1916
War Diary	Albert	10/09/1916	14/09/1916
War Diary	Bernafay	14/09/1916	14/09/1916
War Diary	W of Delville	15/09/1916	17/09/1916
War Diary	Epagne	01/09/1916	01/09/1916
War Diary	Ailly	02/09/1916	02/09/1916
War Diary	Dernancourt	03/09/1916	03/09/1916
War Diary	Albert	10/09/1916	10/09/1916
War Diary	Shlanguval	10/09/1916	10/09/1916
War Diary	Albert	12/09/1916	12/09/1916
War Diary	Sh. Longueval	14/09/1916	14/09/1916
War Diary	Shlanguval	17/09/1916	17/09/1916
War Diary	Trenches	17/09/1916	17/09/1916
War Diary	Shloquert	24/09/1916	24/09/1916
War Diary	Pont Remy	01/09/1916	01/09/1916
War Diary	Ailly Sur Somme	02/09/1916	02/09/1916
War Diary	Dernacourt	10/09/1916	10/09/1916
War Diary	Albert	15/09/1916	15/09/1916
War Diary	E. 18. A. 10.8	19/09/1916	19/09/1916
War Diary		01/10/1916	31/10/1916
War Diary		01/10/1916	07/10/1916
War Diary		08/10/1916	14/10/1916
War Diary		18/10/1916	31/10/1916
War Diary		02/10/1916	31/10/1916
War Diary		13/10/1916	13/10/1916
War Diary		01/10/1916	01/10/1916
War Diary	S.W of Longueval	01/10/1916	31/10/1916
War Diary	Mametz	01/10/1916	31/10/1916
War Diary	Albert	31/10/1916	31/10/1916
War Diary	Combined Sheet 57 d SE.57c S.W. 62 d NE. 62c NW	02/10/1916	02/10/1916
War Diary	S 6. c.77	02/10/1916	31/10/1916
War Diary	S. 16.d.12	09/10/1916	16/10/1916
War Diary	Sh. Longueval	01/10/1916	31/10/1916
War Diary	S.16.d 72 (Albert) Combined Sheet 57d SE 57. SW 62 d N.E. 62 c N.W.	01/10/1916	30/10/1916
War Diary	S. 6.c 77	01/10/1916	30/10/1916
War Diary	Mametz	31/10/1916	31/10/1916
War Diary	Le Meuville	08/11/1916	08/11/1916
War Diary	Mac Becque	09/11/1916	09/11/1916
War Diary	Reninghelst.	12/11/1916	12/11/1916
War Diary	Dickebusch	12/11/1916	25/11/1916
War Diary	Mametz	31/10/1916	31/10/1916
War Diary	Le Neuville	08/11/1916	08/11/1916
War Diary	Morbecque	09/11/1916	09/11/1916

War Diary	Dickebusch	12/11/1916	30/11/1916
War Diary		16/11/1916	16/11/1916
War Diary	Mametz	31/10/1916	31/10/1916
War Diary	Le Neuville	08/11/1916	08/11/1916
War Diary	Morbecque	09/11/1916	09/11/1916
War Diary	Dickebusch.	12/11/1916	29/11/1916
War Diary		25/11/1916	25/11/1916
War Diary	Mametz	31/10/1916	31/10/1916
War Diary	La Neuville	31/10/1916	31/10/1916
War Diary	Morbec	08/11/1916	08/11/1916
War Diary	Reninghelst	09/11/1916	09/11/1916
War Diary	Dickebusch	12/11/1916	12/11/1916
War Diary	St Eloi	12/11/1916	29/11/1916
War Diary	Dickebusch	01/12/1916	31/12/1916
War Diary	Dickebusch	01/12/1916	30/12/1916
War Diary	St. Eloi	01/12/1916	28/12/1916
War Diary	Dickebusch.	01/12/1916	31/12/1916
War Diary	Dickebusch.	01/01/1917	16/01/1917
War Diary		12/01/1917	31/01/1917
War Diary		13/01/1917	13/01/1917
War Diary	St Eloi	01/01/1917	31/01/1917
War Diary	Diependaal	07/01/1917	30/01/1917
War Diary		28/01/1917	31/01/1917
War Diary	Dickebusch	01/01/1917	31/01/1917
War Diary	Dickebusch	01/01/1917	23/02/1917
War Diary	St Eloi	01/02/1917	28/02/1917
War Diary	Wytschaete	01/02/1917	28/02/1917
War Diary	Dickebusch	01/02/1917	23/02/1917
War Diary	Dickebusch	01/02/1917	31/03/1917
War Diary	St. Eloi	01/03/1917	31/03/1917
War Diary	Dickebusch	01/03/1917	25/04/1917
War Diary	Dickebusch	23/04/1917	25/04/1917
War Diary	St Eloi	25/04/1917	25/04/1917
War Diary	Dickebusch	01/04/1917	31/05/1917
War Diary	Dickebusch	08/05/1917	08/05/1917
War Diary	St Eloi	08/05/1917	08/05/1917
War Diary	Dickebush	01/05/1917	30/06/1917
War Diary	St Eloi	30/06/1917	30/06/1917
War Diary	Dickebusch	01/06/1917	05/07/1917
War Diary	Boeschepe	12/07/1917	19/07/1917
War Diary	Dickebusch	23/07/1917	29/07/1917
War Diary	Dickebusch H 31 d 8 1/2	01/07/1917	05/07/1917
War Diary	Boeschepe R 15 a 0.3	05/07/1917	23/07/1917
War Diary	Dickebusch N 1 b 2.5	23/07/1917	31/07/1917
War Diary	Dickebusch.	01/08/1917	31/08/1917
War Diary	Dickebusch N.1 b 2.5.	01/08/1917	30/09/1917
War Diary	Dickebusch N 1 b 2.5	01/09/1917	02/09/1917
War Diary	Boeschepe R 10 d 8.2	02/09/1917	13/09/1917
War Diary	Dickebusch N.3 b 2.4	13/09/1917	30/09/1917
War Diary	Dickebusch	01/10/1917	07/10/1917
War Diary	Dunkirk St. Pol	07/10/1917	07/10/1917
War Diary	Coxyde Bains	12/10/1917	12/10/1917
War Diary	Ghyvelde	29/10/1917	29/10/1917

41ST DIVISION

TRENCH MORTAR BATTS.

MAY 1916-~~OCT 1918~~ OCT 1917
MAR 1918 - OCT 1918

ITALY 1917 NOV - 1918 FEB

WO95/2625/7

41 DIV

DIV TRENCH MORTAR BATTERY

MAY 1916 - OCT 1917

Secret – XLI

Instructions regarding War Diaries and Intelligence Summaries are contained in F. S. Regs., Part II, and the Staff Manual respectively. Title pages will be prepared in manuscript.

TRENCH MORTAR BATTERIES. 41 DIVN.

WAR DIARY

or

~~INTELLIGENCE SUMMARY.~~

(Erase heading not required.)

Army Form C. 2118.

X.Y.Z.41.

Vol 1

Place	Date	Hour	Summary of Events and Information	Remarks and references to Appendices
Sheet 38 B.23 d 48	17-5-16		The three Medium Trench Mortar Batteries, 41 DIVN, were formed – HQS being at B.23.d 48 (Sheet 36). The Officers, N.C.O's, & men for the same being obtained from the B.A.C's.	X/41 Y/41 Z/41
	17-5-16 to 25-5-16		The Medium 2" T.M. Btys, referred to above, were attached to the 9th DIV T.M. Btys for instruction in the line. U 14 b 95 – C 16 b 65 (Sheet 36)	
	25-5-16		V/41 Heavy T.M. By formed, not up to full strength.	
	26-5-16 to 31-5-16		Work in progress on defensive emplacements in the line, the 41 DIV T M Btys having taken over from 9th DIV T M Btys on 26th. A few rounds were fired to register our own front line in certain places.	
			31-5-16.	
			[signature] Capt R.F.A. T.M.C. 41 DIV ARTY	

2353 Wt. W2544/1454 700,000 5/15 D. D. & L. A.D.S.S. Forms/C. 2118.

8

I753

CONFIDENTIAL

D.A.G.,
3rd. Echelon,
B A S E.

Herewith true copy of War Diary from D.T.M.O., 41st.Division, called for in your No.121/9020 (A.G.1.) of the 31st.May last.

H E McKie 2/Lt
for Colonel, R.A.
Commanding 41st.Divisional Artill

4.7.17

Instructions regarding War Diaries and Intelligence Summaries are contained in F. S. Regs., Part II. and the Staff Manual respectively. Title pages will be prepared in manuscript.

WAR DIARY
or
INTELLIGENCE SUMMARY.
(Erase heading not required.)

41 T M Bty

Army Form C. 2118.

Vol I

Place	Date	Hour	Summary of Events and Information	Remarks and references to Appendices
	29/5/16		Moved from the BOIS DES ALLEUX to the CHATEAU at ECOIVRES. Reserve personnel proceeded to 3rd Army School of Mortars to form 41/2 T.M.B. TAB	
	10/6/16		41/2. T.M.B arrive back from the School of Mortars LIGNY. TAB	
	12/6/16		41/1 & 41/2. T.M.Btys formed into 41st T.M.Bty. TAB	
	20/6/16	9 p.m	Moved from the CHATEAU at ECOIVRES to ARRAS arriving at 1.a.m on the night of 20/21st inst. TAB	
	22/6/16.		Sent 8 mortars to a cellar at ROCLINCOURT with a guard TAB	
	23/6/16		Four guns go into action on the right of K I sector TAB	
	24/6/16		94 rounds fired on enemy front line in retaliation for enemy Grenades and rifle bombs and heavy minenwerfers. Generally two rounds were fired to every one	
	25/6/16	11.8 pm	41st T.M.B with 6 guns on the right fired rapidly for 2 minutes in conjunction with artillery bombardment. 6 guns were in position to fire Rate of fire 12 rounds a minute. TAB	
		11.30 pm	Stokes gun opened fire again for one minute. Retaliation was not severe. Total rounds fired by the battery during combined bombardment 188 TAB	
	26/6/16	4 pm – 7 pm	105 rounds fired in retaliation for heavy enemy mortars which fired about 30 or 40 rounds Enemy also retaliated with 77 cm QF TAB	

1577 Wt. W10791/1773 500,000 1/15 D. D. & L. A.D.S.S./Forms/C. 2118.

Instructions regarding War Diaries and Intelligence Summaries are contained in F. S. Regs., Part II. and the Staff Manual respectively. Title pages will be prepared in manuscript.

WAR DIARY
or
INTELLIGENCE SUMMARY.
(Erase heading not required.)

Army Form C. 2118.

Place	Date	Hour	Summary of Events and Information	Remarks and references to Appendices
	27/6/16	Appro 4 pm	4 guns are put into ~~line in place of~~ positions vacated by 13/1 & 13/2. T.M. Btries TAB	
	28/6/16	5.7 pm	Combined bombardment on K Sector 5.7 pm. All Trench Mortars fire rapidly for two	
		5.23 pm	minutes. ie. 41st T.M. Bty (8 guns) 15/2. T.M Bty (2 guns) 5.23. All Trench Mortars fire rapidly for one minute. Total fire by 41st Bty. 288. Rate of fire 12 rounds per minute. 15/2. T.M Bty fire 71 rounds. TAB.	
	29/6/16	7.0 pm	Right Gun in VICTORIA STREET registers with 4 shots from new Emplacement. Enemy retaliate with 3 mortars.	
		8.0 pm	Left two guns register 10 rounds from emplacements vacated by 15/2. T.M. Bty on the night of the 28/29th. TAB	
	30/6/16		Work carried on in refitting emplacements TAB	

T.A. Baldock 2Lt

OC 41st T.M.B & K Sector Mortars.

30/6/16

1577 Wt. W10791/1773 500,000 1/15 D. D. & L. A.D.S.S./Forms/C. 2118.

Secret

Instructions regarding War Diaries and Intelligence Summaries are contained in F. S. Regs., Part II. and the Staff Manual respectively. Title Pages will be prepared in manuscript.

WAR DIARY
or
~~INTELLIGENCE SUMMARY~~ TRENCH MORTAR BATTERIES.
41st DIVISION.

(Erase heading not required.)

Army Form. C. 2118

Vol II

Place	Date	Hour	Summary of Events and Information	Remarks and references to Appendices
SHEET. 28 S.W.	8/6/16		Six Medium 2" Trench Mortars belonging to X. Y. Z. Batteries (2 Mortars from each Battery) and firing from positions approx. as shown	
U.27 d 9.9 U.27 b 9.6.		3.10 pm to 3.45 pm	assisted in an Artillery bombardment of "THE FORT" U.28.a 5.6. Rounds fired 124. Result satisfactory. Registration done previously. Casualties and damages sustained nil.	
C. 4. a ½ .6.	30/6/16		Two Mortars of X/41 Trench Mortar Battery successfully cut wire in front of German Trenches for use of night raiding party about C 4 a 8.2 during the morning; and at night took part in Artillery bombardments before the raid firing on German front line. Emplacements heavily shelled by 4.2"s and 77's and badly damaged. Casualties 2 N.C.O's wounded. Certain damage to material sustained.	
U.27 d 9.9 U.27 b 9.6			Two Mortars of X/41 and four Mortars from Y/41 cut wire during day and afterwards bombarded at night "THE FORT" and German trenches about U.28. a.5.6. Very good shooting made. Emplacements subject	

Army Form. C. 2118

Instructions regarding War Diaries and Intelligence Summaries are contained in F. S. Regs., Part II. and the Staff Manual respectively. Title Pages will be prepared in manuscript.

WAR DIARY

or

~~INTELLIGENCE SUMMARY~~

(Erase heading not required.)

Place	Date	Hour	Summary of Events and Information	Remarks and references to Appendices
			to very heavy bombardment of 5.9"s, 4.2"s. 77s, three of them being put out of action, by end of the operations, by direct hits of 5.9"s and 4.2"s.	
			Casualties 1 man Killed, 1 Officer, 2 N.C.O's, 4 men wounded. Much damage to material sustained.	
			In one emplacement a 5.9" set fire to some of the cordite charges and some Ammunition was damaged before the fire could be got under.	
U. 15 c 5½. 9 U. 15 d 0. 4½	30/6/16		4 Mortars Z/41 cut wire about U.15 d 7¾. 6. and afterwards took part in preliminary bombardment of German trenches before Infantry raids, with success. Casualties and damage sustained, Nil. 1 Rifle mechanism blew out of Mortar after 106 rounds.	
			Registration for this operation was done during previous days.	
			Rounds used in operation 1044.	
			Rounds used during Month in operations, registration, etc = 1208.	
			3.7.16 J. Longbourne. Capt R.F.A. T.M.C. 41st Division	

5,000 — Imp. des A. C. — 24.7.15

1/

Instructions regarding War Diaries and Intelligence Summaries are contained in F. S. Regs., Part II. and the Staff Manual respectively. Title pages will be prepared in manuscript.

WAR DIARY
or
~~INTELLIGENCE SUMMARY.~~
(Erase heading not required.)

JUNE 1916

TRENCH MORTAR BATTERIES
41 DIVISION.

Army Form C. 2118.

COPY.

41

Vol 4

Place	Date	Hour	Summary of Events and Information	Remarks and references to Appendices
SHEET 28 S.W. U 27 d 9.9 U 27 b 9.6.	8/6/16	3.10 PM to 3.45 PM	Six Medium 2" Trench Mortars belonging to X Y and Z Batteries (2 Mortars from each Battery) and firing from positions approx. as shown assisted in an Artillery bombardment of THE FORT U 28 a 5.6. Rounds fired 124. Result satisfactory. Registration done previously. Casualties and damage sustained Nil.	
C 4 a 2.6	30/6/16		Two Mortars of X/41 Trench Mortar Battery successfully cut wire in front of German trenches for use of night raiding party about C.4 a 8.2. during the morning, and at night took part in Artillery bombardments before the raid, firing on German front line. Emplacements heavily shelled by 4.2's and 77's and badly damaged. Casualties. 2 N.C.O's wounded. Certain damage to material sustained.	
U 27 d 9.9 U 27 b 9.6			Two Mortars of X/41 and four Mortars from Y/41 cut wire during day and afterwards bombarded at night, THE FORT and	

T2134. Wt. W708–776. 500000. 4/15. Sir J. C. & S.

2

Instructions regarding War Diaries and Intelligence Summaries are contained in F. S. Regs., Part II. and the Staff Manual respectively. Title pages will be prepared in manuscript.

WAR DIARY

~~or~~

~~INTELLIGENCE SUMMARY.~~

(Erase heading not required.)

Army Form C. 2118.

Place	Date	Hour	Summary of Events and Information	Remarks and references to Appendices
			German trenches about U 28 a 5.6. Very good shooting made. Emplacements subject to very heavy bombardment of 5.9's, 4.2's and 77's three of them being put out of action, by end of the operations by direct hits of 5.9's and 4.2's.	
			Casualties 1 man Killed, 1 Officer, 2 N.C.O's, and four men wounded. Much damage to material sustained.	
			In one emplacement a 5.9 set fire to some of the cordite charges, and some ammunition was damaged before the fire could be got under.	
U 15 c 5½.9. U 15 d 0.4½	30/6/16		4 Mortars Z/41 cut wire about U 15 d. 7¾ 6. and afterwards took part in preliminary bombardment of German trenches before Infantry raids with success. Casualties and damage sustained, Nil. 1 Rifle Mechanism blew out of Mortar after 106 rounds.	
			Registration for this operation was done during previous days.	
			Rounds used in operation 1044.	
			Rounds used during month in operations registration etc. — 1208.	
			(Signed) J Longbourne, Capt. R.F.A. T.M.C. 41 Division	

T2134. Wt. W708—776. 500000. 4/15. Sir J. C. & S.

3.7.16

SECRET

Instructions regarding War Diaries and Intelligence Summaries are contained in F. S. Regs., Part II. and the Staff Manual respectively. Title Pages will be prepared in manuscript.

WAR DIARY or ~~INTELLIGENCE SUMMARY~~

(Erase heading not required.)

I. HEAVY AND MEDIUM TRENCH MORTAR BATTERIES. 41 DIVISION

41 July

Army Form C. 2118.

Vol 5

Place	Date	Hour	Summary of Events and Information	Remarks and references to Appendices
SHEET 28 S.W. U.15. d.0.4½	4.7.16	10.40 p.m.	Two 2" Trench Mortars of Z/41 Trench Mortar Battery fired 14 rounds on German Trench and wire about U.15 d.7¾.6 where enemy were carrying out repairs in retaliation for hostile Trench Mortars.	
U.15 d.0.4½ U.15 d.1.5½	8.7.16	MORNING 8 am to 1 pm	Four 2" Trench Mortars of Z/41 Trench Mortar Battery in action as shown in margin employed in cutting wire for use of Infantry raiding party from U.15. d. 9¼.4. to U.15 d. 9.4½. This was successfully done despite very heavy hostile retaliation from 5.9's Trench Mortars and other weapons which did great damage all round emplacements without actually hitting them.	
			Casualties. 1 Man wounded. Rounds fired 200.	
U.14 b	10.7.16	MORNING 9.11am	Took over 2 positions in bad condition from 24th Division Trench Mortars in square U.15. b. Moved 1 section Z/41 from U.15. d. to this position.	
U.15. d.0.4½	12.7.16	8 am to 12 NOON	Two 2" Trench Mortars Z/41 Trench Mortar Battery occupied in "dud" wire cutting about U.15 d.8.6. to U.15 d.9.7. as a blind, in connection with	

2449 Wt. W14957/M90 750,000 1/16 J.B.C. & A. Forms/C.2118/12.

II

Army Form C. 2118.

WAR DIARY
or
~~INTELLIGENCE SUMMARY~~
(Erase heading not required.)

Instructions regarding War Diaries and Intelligence Summaries are contained in F. S. Regs., Part II. and the Staff Manual respectively. Title Pages will be prepared in manuscript.

Place	Date	Hour	Summary of Events and Information	Remarks and references to Appendices
			a raid by Infantry.	
			A premature occurred at one Mortar Killing one gunner, and wounding one N.C.O and two gunners and the allowance of 40 rounds had to be fired by the remaining Mortar, with retaliation of 4·2's, and ·77's.	
U.15 d 0.4½ U.15 d 1.5½	14.7.16	8 AM TO 12 NOON	One Trench Mortar X/41, one Trench Mortar Y/41, and one Trench Mortar Z/41 in action, position as shown, occupied in cutting wire U.15 d 8.8½ to U.15 d 8½ 9¼ in connection with an Infantry raid. This was carried out in conjunction with 18 pounders quite satisfactorily under very heavy fire of 4·2's and 5·9's, one gun being put out of action half way through owing to two direct hits of 5·9's on front of the emplacement blocking the working of the Mortar.	
			Casualties Nil. Rounds fired 138.	
U.27 b 8½.1	16.7.16	8 AM to 12.30 pm	Two 2" Trench Mortars of Y/41 engaged in firing short bursts of 5 rounds on enemy salient about U 28 a 4.8 where Machine Gun emplacements were known. Hostile retaliation ~~not~~ over heavy, until some	

2449 Wt. W14957/M90 750,000 1/16 J.B.C. & A. Forms/C.2118/12.

III

Army Form C. 2118.

WAR DIARY
or
~~INTELLIGENCE SUMMARY~~
(Erase heading not required.)

Instructions regarding War Diaries and Intelligence Summaries are contained in F. S. Regs., Part II. and the Staff Manual respectively. Title Pages will be prepared in manuscript.

Place	Date	Hour	Summary of Events and Information	Remarks and references to Appendices
			time after Trench Mortars had ceased, when a section of 5.9's shelled our trenches considerably in the vicinity. Casualties, Nil. Rounds fired 35.	
U 15 d 1.5½	16.7.16	11 Am to 1 pm.	Two 2" Trench Mortars Z/41 fired 20 rounds in bursts of 5 rounds on hostile trenches U.15 b 8.0, U.15 b 81, U 15. d 8½. 8½. and U 15 d 8.6. Hostile retaliation chiefly 4.2's; one hit obtained on an emplacement but doing no serious damage. Casualties. Nil.	
Sheet 36.N.W. C4. c 7.7¼	24.7.16	5.30 pm to 8.30 pm	Two 2" Trench Mortars X/41 in action as shown, being employed in cutting wire for Infantry raid between points C4 d 22 and C4 d 1½. 4½ and hostile front line to assist 18 pounders. This was carried out in two bursts of fire, 25 rounds per Mortar per burst; 100 rounds in all. Retaliation 77's and Trench Mortars, but good emplacement saved detachments. Casualties, Nil.	

2449 Wt. W14957/M90 750,000 1/16 J.B.C. & A. Forms/C.2118/12.

IV

Army Form C. 2118.

WAR DIARY
or
~~INTELLIGENCE SUMMARY~~
(Erase heading not required.)

Instructions regarding War Diaries and Intelligence Summaries are contained in F. S. Regs., Part II. and the Staff Manual respectively. Title Pages will be prepared in manuscript.

Place	Date	Hour	Summary of Events and Information	Remarks and references to Appendices
SHEET 28. S.W. U27 b. 8½.1	24.7.16	4.20 pm to 7.15 pm	Two 2" Trench Mortars Y/41 engaged in dud cutting wire U28 a 4.8 to U28 a 3½. 8½ as a blind preparatory to an Infantry raid. After 48 rounds fire had to be stopped despite strong emplacements owing to lack of covering fire and severe hostile retaliation consisting of 5.9s, 4.2's and 77's. One pit hit four times, the other once. Casualties Nil.	
U 21 a 7.7.		4 pm.	240 m.m. V/41 in action as shown fired one round on hostile front line U 15 d. 9.4½.	
		7.5 pm	240 m.m. V/41 in action as shown, fired one round on hostile supports U.15 d 10.5.	
U 15 d 1.5½	25.7.16		Two 2" Trench Mortars Z/41 Trench Mortar Battery fired 30 rounds on to hostile trenches U.15 d 8½. 8. and U.15. d. 8½.7 while wire cutting was going on by 18 pounders doing considerable damage. The usual retaliation followed in due course, one Mortar pit being hit by 4.2	

2449 Wt. W14957/M90 750,000 1/16 J.B.C. & A. Forms/C.2118/12.

V

Instructions regarding War Diaries and Intelligence Summaries are contained in F. S. Regs., Part II. and the Staff Manual respectively. Title Pages will be prepared in manuscript.

WAR DIARY
or
~~INTELLIGENCE SUMMARY~~
(Erase heading not required.)

Army Form C. 2118.

Place	Date	Hour	Summary of Events and Information	Remarks and references to Appendices
			without doing much damage.	
			Casualties Nil.	
SHEET 28. S.W. U 27 b 8½.1.	25.7.16	5.30 pm to 6.30 pm	Two 2" Trench Mortars Y/41 completed wire cutting, starting on the 24th from U 15 d 8½.8. to U 15 d 8½.7. firing 50 rounds with success. Hostile retaliation came an hour later, an hostile aeroplane ranging two 5.9's and a Battery of 4.2's on the emplacements one of which was practically blotted out by numerous hits. The men got clear of the gun and were removed to a spare pit of equal strength.	
			Casualties Nil.	
U 21 a 7.7		4.10 pm	240 m.m. V/41 in action as shown fired one round on hostile trenches about U 15 d 10.5.	
		7.30 pm	240 m.m. V/41 in action as shown fired one round on hostile trenches about U 15 d 10.5	
			Casualties. One man wounded in O.P.	

2449 Wt. W14957/M90 750,000 1/16 J.B.C. & A. Forms/C.2118/12.

VI

Army Form C. 2118.

WAR DIARY
or
~~INTELLIGENCE SUMMARY~~
(Erase heading not required.)

Instructions regarding War Diaries and Intelligence Summaries are contained in F. S. Regs., Part II. and the Staff Manual respectively. Title Pages will be prepared in manuscript.

Place	Date	Hour	Summary of Events and Information	Remarks and references to Appendices
SHEET 36 N.W. C 4 c 7.7¼	26.7.16	6 pm to 6.30 pm	Two 2" Trench Mortars X/41 fired 50 rounds on wire as pointed out by O/c "Raids" about C 4 d 2 2 in connection with Infantry raid that night.	
		11 pm to 12	Took part in bombardment. Fired on front hostile trench C 4 d 2.4½. C 4 d 3¼.3 with special reference to Machine Gun emplacement at C 4 d 2¼ 3¾ with apparent success. Machine Gun in question was not troublesome during raid. Rounds fired 55, average approx. one per minute.	
			Casualties, one man wounded in O.P. during wire cutting.	
SHEET 28.S.W U 27 b 8½.1	26.7.16	11-12 p.m.	Two 2" Trench Mortars Y/41, took part in bombardment, their target being the angle of hostile trench contained by U 28 a 4 8, U 28 a 3½.8½, U 28 a 4.9.	
		12 MIDNIGHT TO 12-40 am	Continued to form barrage about U 28 a 5½.9½, to U 28 a 4.8½, while raid took place. Rounds fired 91, average just under one per minute.	

2449 Wt. W14957/M90 750,000 1/16 J.B.C. & A. Forms/C.2118/12.

VII

Instructions regarding War Diaries and Intelligence Summaries are contained in F. S. Regs., Part II. and the Staff Manual respectively. Title Pages will be prepared in manuscript.

WAR DIARY
or
~~INTELLIGENCE SUMMARY~~
(Erase heading not required.)

Army Form C. 2118.

Place	Date	Hour	Summary of Events and Information	Remarks and references to Appendices
			Operation apparently quite successful.	
			Casualties Nil. Emplacements coming off lightly in general bombardment	
U21 a 7.7.		4-45 pm. 7-56 pm 11-1 pm 11-15 pm 11-29 pm	One round 240 m.m. V/41 fired at the time shown, the last three under cover of smoke clouds put out by Infantry for 3 periods of 2 minutes each at intervals of 12 minutes which was quite successful in hiding flash. Rounds fell in trenches about U 16 c 1.6, U 16 c 12.5, U 16. c 4.7, U 16. c 4.8. doing considerable damage as far as could be seen, next day.	
			Total rounds fired during month. { 240 m.m. 9 rounds. " " " " { 2" 871 "	
			Total Casualties. 1 Man Killed, 2 N.C.O's and 8 other ranks wounded during period under consideration as well as in operations as above.	

J. Longbourne Capt. R.F.A.
T.M.O. 41st DIV.
31-7-16.

2449 Wt. W14957/M90 750,000 1/16 J.B.C. & A. Forms/C.2118/12.

Instructions regarding War Diaries and Intelligence Summaries are contained in F. S. Regs., Part II. and the Staff Manual respectively. Title Pages will be prepared in manuscript.

WAR DIARY
or
~~INTELLIGENCE SUMMARY~~
(Erase heading not required.)

Army Form C. 2118.

V026

HEAVY AND MEDIUM TRENCH MORTAR BATTERIES 41 DIVISION

Place	Date	Hour	Summary of Events and Information	Remarks and references to Appendices
Sheet 28 S.W.	7-8/8/16		Removed the two Mortars from defensive positions in V.14.b. to original positions in V.15.b. belonging to Z/41 T.M.B.	
41st Div. front.	23/8/16	5 pm	V Heavy Trench Mortar Battery, and X. Y. Z. Trench Mortar Batteries position and registration were handed over to 23rd Division.	
			During the period under review, no offensive or defensive operations were carried out. There was very little Trench Mortar activity on the part of the enemy during this time.	
			Number of rounds expended Nil.	
			Number of Casualties. 1 N.C.O. 1 man.	
			Jesse H. Hill Lieut. RHA of T.M.C. 41st Division.	

Instructions regarding War Diaries and Intelligence Summaries are contained in F. S. Regs., Part II. and the Staff Manual respectively. Title Pages will be prepared in manuscript.

WAR DIARY or ~~INTELLIGENCE SUMMARY~~

(Erase heading not required.)

TRENCH MORTAR BATTERIES 41 DIVISION. Vol 7

Army Form C. 2118.

Place	Date	Hour	Summary of Events and Information	Remarks and references to Appendices
EPAGNE	1.9.16		X Y and Z Trench Mortar Batteries left Epagne and proceeded to Ailly. V Heavy Trench Mortar Battery left Pont Remy and proceeded with Medium Trench Mortar Batteries.	
AILLY	2.9.16		Medium and Heavy Trench Mortar Batteries proceeded to Dernancourt where they billetted until the 10 inst.	
DERNANCOURT	10.9.16		On the morning of the 10th inst. the Divisional front was reconnoitred for positions, and to bring Heavy or Medium Batteries into action. Was found impossible either to get guns up, or to find definite target. On the 10th inst. Batteries moved up and bivouacked near Albert. Training was carried out by all Batteries at this point. Medium Batteries moved up to Delville Wood and remained in reserve until the 17th inst. when they moved back to Mametz.	
	17-24		The personnel of Batteries were employed assisting 18 pr and 4.5 guns.	
	24		Medium Batteries again moved up to Delville Wood, and remained in reserve until the 28th inst.	
	28-30		Personnel of Batteries was sent to assist 18 pr and 4.5 guns into line. Rounds fired. Nil. Casualties. 1 N.C.O. died of wounds. ~~and~~ 2 gunners wounded.	

J. A. Hill, Capt. R.F.A.
T.M.C. 41 Division

2449 Wt. W14957/M90 750,000 1/16 J.B.C. & A. Forms/C.2118/12.

Instructions regarding War Diaries and Intelligence Summaries are contained in F. S. Regs., Part II. and the Staff Manual respectively. Title Pages will be prepared in manuscript.

WAR DIARY ~~or~~ ~~INTELLIGENCE SUMMARY~~

(Erase heading not required.)

Y/41 TRENCH MORTAR BATTERY

Army Form C. 2118.

Place	Date	Hour	Summary of Events and Information	Remarks and references to Appendices
Epagne	1/9/16		The battery left Epagne & proceeded to Ailly, where they billeted for the night.	
Ailly	[illegible]/9/16		Left Ailly for Bernancourt, where they bivouaced & continued training till 10/9/16.	
Albert	10/9/16		A position for battery was reconnoitred by the B.C. along the Div. front, but it was found impossible to come into action. The Battery moved into bivouacs near Albert.	
"	12/9/16		The battery moved into a reserve position at S.22.b.79 near Delville Wood, & relieved X/41.	
W. of Delville Wood S22b79	13/9/16		Dugouts were built & 100 complete rounds brought from Green Dump to position.	
"	14/9/16		Remainder of Brigade joined the Battery at Reserve position.	
Mametz	17/9/16		Left reserve position with Bde. & moved back near Mametz F5 b 1½ 2½.	
"	19/9/16		Battery split up into working parties for the 187 & 189 Bde. R.F.A. returning each night to bivouac at F5 b 3½ 2½. till 23/9/16.	
S22b79.	23/9/16		Battery again proceeded to Reserve position at S22b79 with remainder of Bde.	
"	28/9/16		Working parties again proceeded to the 187 & 189 Bdes R.F.A till the end of the month. On 28/9/16 the B.C. Lt. Harris left the battery to take command of C/189.	

R.W. Burns [illegible]
2/Lt. R.F.A.
Y/41 T.M.B.

2449 Wt. W14957/M90 750,000 1/16 J.B.C. & A. Forms/C.2118/12.

Instructions regarding War Diaries and Intelligence Summaries are contained in F. S. Regs., Part II. and the Staff Manual respectively. Title Pages will be prepared in manuscript.

WAR DIARY
or
~~INTELLIGENCE SUMMARY~~
(Erase heading not required.)

X/41 TRENCH MORTAR BATTERY.

Army Form C. 2118.

Place	Date	Hour	Summary of Events and Information	Remarks and references to Appendices
Mametz	Sept. 17th – 24th		Moved back to position near Mametz (F 5 b 3½ 2½) & went into bivouac where it remained until Sept 24th. From 19th – 23rd the personnel of the battery was employed in fatigue work for 183rd Bdge. R.F.A.	
W. of Delville	Sept 24th – 30th		Moved back to F 5 b 3½ 2½ & again remained there in reserve. The personnel of the battery was sent to assist F.A. batteries of the Division on Sept. 28th & 29th.	

F. A. Rushbrooke 2/Lt. RFA
O. C. X/41 T.M.B.

2449 Wt. W14957/M90 750,000 1/16 J.B.C. & A. Forms/C.2118/12.

Instructions regarding War Diaries and Intelligence Summaries are contained in F. S. Regs., Part II. and the Staff Manual respectively. Title Pages will be prepared in manuscript.

WAR DIARY

~~or~~

~~INTELLIGENCE SUMMARY~~

(Erase heading not required.)

X/41 TRENCH MORTAR BATTERY

Army Form C. 2118.

Place	Date	Hour	Summary of Events and Information	Remarks and references to Appendices
Epagne	1 Sept		The Battery left Epagne & proceeded by lorry to Ailly.	
Ailly	2 Sept		Continued the journey to Dernancourt, bivouacing just outside the village.	
Dernancourt	3rd – 10th		Remained in bivouac & continued training programme.	
			On the early morning of the 10th the acting B.C. (in company with the T.M.O. & the other two B.Cs.) went up to reconnoitre the Divisional front along Delville Wood to ascertain whether it would be possible to get the guns into position for wire cutting in front of Switch Trench. It was found that in the then unconsolidated state of the trenches it was absolutely impossible to get the guns & necessary stores up near enough to the target.	
	10th	2 pm	The Battery left bivouac & proceeded to a new bivouac near Albert in G.S. waggons provided by No 4 Section – D.A.C.	
Albert	10th – 14th		Remained in bivouac, the men being employed in training & general fatigues.	
Bernafay	14th		The Battery was detailed to proceed to Bernafay Quarry to take over an ammunition dump & to act as reserve for the remainder of the Brigade.	
W. of Delville	15th – 17th		The Battery, taking 20 complete rounds moved up to join the remainder at S 22 B 7 9, W. of Delville Wood, remaining there until 17th in reserve, but it was not found possible to make use of the mortars.	

2449 Wt. W14957/M90 750,000 1/16 J.B.C. & A. Forms/C.2118/12.

Instructions regarding War Diaries and Intelligence Summaries are contained in F. S. Regs., Part II. and the Staff Manual respectively. Title Pages will be prepared in manuscript.

WAR DIARY
or
INTELLIGENCE SUMMARY
(Erase heading not required.)

2/41 TRENCH MORTAR BATTERY

Army Form C. 2118.

Place	Date	Hour	Summary of Events and Information	Remarks and references to Appendices
Epagne	1/9/16		The battery with others of the Brigade left Epagne in the [illegible] and billeted for the night at Ailly.	
Ailly	2/9/16		Leaving Ailly the battery proceeded as before by motor lorry to Dernancourt, bivouaced there, and continued training etc from the 3rd to the 10th inst.	
Dernancourt	3/9/16		On the morning of the 10th the O.C. in company with the T.M.O. and the other B.Cs proceeded through Delville Wood to the front line trenches to reconnoitre a position for the battery, with a view to engaging as a target the Switch trench [illegible] at S 6 c. It was however found impossible to bring the battery into action.	
Albert	10/9/16		On the afternoon of the 10th the Brigade moved to Albert and the battery was detailed to take up a reserve position at S22 b 7.9 where bomb stores etc were prepared.	
[illegible] Longueval	10/9/16			
Albert	12/9/16		On the 12th inst the battery was relieved by Y battery and returned to Albert.	
[illegible] Longueval	14/9/16		The battery with others of the Brigade moved into the reserve position at S22 b 7.9 and reported to O.C. C battery 183rd Brigade, remaining in communication with ~~[illegible]~~ line	

2449 Wt. W14957/M90 750,000 1/16 J.B.C. & A. Forms/C.2118/12.

Instructions regarding War Diaries and Intelligence Summaries are contained in F. S. Regs., Part II. and the Staff Manual respectively. Title Pages will be prepared in manuscript.

WAR DIARY
or
INTELLIGENCE SUMMARY
(Erase heading not required.)

Army Form C. 2118.

Place	Date	Hour	Summary of Events and Information	Remarks and references to Appendices
Longueval	17/9/16		On the 17th the battery was instructed to report to the H.Q. D.A.C. at Mametz, & bivouacs at F5 c 3½ 2½.	
Mametz	19/9/16		From the 19th to the 23rd inst inclusive the personnel of the battery was employed at H.Q. 190th Brigade Delville Wood returning each evening to the bivouacs at F5 c 3½ 2½.	
			On the 22nd & 23rd inst the officers of the battery were attached for duty to the D.A.C.	
Longueval	24/9/16		The battery again moved into reserve position at S22 b 7.9 & remained here until the 30th: it was again found impossible to engage a target during the period. [illegible]	
			Number of rounds fired during period under review nil	
			Casualties	
			Bbr Russell Died of wounds	
			40287 Gnr Day Wounded	
			R. S. Perry Lt RGA.	
			O.C. [illegible] T.M.B.	

2149 Wt. W14957/M90 750,000 1/16 J.B.C. & A. Forms/C.2118/12.

Instructions regarding War Diaries and Intelligence Summaries are contained in F. S. Regs., Part II. and the Staff Manual respectively. Title Pages will be prepared in manuscript.

WAR DIARY ~~or~~ ~~INTELLIGENCE SUMMARY~~

(Erase heading not required.)

V/41 HEAVY TRENCH MORTAR BATTERY.

Army Form C. 2118.

Place	Date	Hour	Summary of Events and Information	Remarks and references to Appendices
			movements	
Pont Remy	1/9/16.	8 pm.	Left for Ailly sur Somme (Billets).	
Ailly sur-Somme.	2/9/16	5 pm.	" " Dernacourt (Bivouac).	
Dernacourt	10/9/16	5 pm.	" Albert (Bivouac).	
Albert	15/9/16	4.30 pm	" Albert and attached B Echelon 41 D A C at E.18.A.10.8. (map ALBERT 1/40000).	
E.18.A.10.8.	19/9/16.	10 AM.	" for Mametz Cemetery.	
			Operations for above period NIL.	
			G Hawkes Capt R.G.A. Comdg V/41 H.T.M Bty.	

2449 Wt. W14957/M90 750,000 1/16 J.B.C. & A. Forms/C.2118/12.

Instructions regarding War Diaries and Intelligence Summaries are contained in F. S. Regs., Part II. and the Staff Manual respectively. Title Pages will be prepared in manuscript.

WAR DIARY
or
INTELLIGENCE SUMMARY
(Erase heading not required.)

V/41 HEAVY TRENCH MORTAR BATTERY.

Army Form C. 2118.

Place	Date	Hour	Summary of Events and Information	Remarks and references to Appendices
	1/10/16 - 31/10/16		4 N.C.O. + 18 men attached to 189th Bdge R.F.A.	
	1/10/16 - 7/10/16		4 N.C.O. + 17 men attached to 189 Bdge R.F.A.	
	8/10/16 - 14/10/16		4 N.C.O. + 17 men " " 41st Ammunition Dump	
	18/10/16 - 31/10/16			
	2/10/16 - 31/10/16		5 men attached to H.Q. Div Arty. Has telephonists + one as Orderly	
	13-10-16		Capt Oakes temporarily attached + to take command of D/183rd Bdge R.F.A.	
	1-10-16		2/Lieut Bavin takes over command of V/41. H.T.M. Batty.	
			A. H. Hudson 2/Lieut. R.F.A. o/c V/41. H.T.M. Batty.	

2449 Wt. W14957/M90 750,000 1/16 J.B.C. & A. Forms/C.2118/12.

Army Form. C. 2118

Instructions regarding War Diaries and Intelligence Summaries are contained in F. S. Regs., Part II. and the Staff Manual respectively. Title Pages will be prepared in manuscript.

WAR DIARY X/41 TRENCH MORTAR BATTERY

or

~~INTELLIGENCE SUMMARY~~

(Erase heading not required.)

OCTOBER 1916 — VOL

Place	Date	Hour	Summary of Events and Information	Remarks and references to Appendices
S.W. of Longueval	Oct 1st – Oct 14th		The men of X Battery embodied in the advanced composite battery were employed during this period in preparing gun positions for the various F.A. Brigades of the Division, in assisting at the Dump & in other fatigue work.	
"	Oct 14th	6.30	Orders were received from the T.M.C. to recall all men of the composite Battery from the Dump & Brigades; to take the 4 guns up to Flers that night, & to select 25 N.C.O's & men to proceed up the line next morning for receiving further instructions. The guns were accordingly taken up to a spot just outside Flers – great difficulty being experienced in this owing to the state of the road – & left there under a guard.	
"	Oct 15th		The personnel of the Battery was held in readiness until 5pm when orders were received cancelling all arrangements & recalling the guns from Flers. – During the night the guns were brought back to their original position.	
"	Oct 15 – Oct 31st		During the remainder of the month the men were employed in general fatigues for Brigades and gun drill.	
Mametz	Oct 1 – 31st		Men of the Battery not included in Advanced Battery remained at Mametz, being employed in ration & other fatigues.	

L. A. Rushbrooke O.C. X/41

Instructions regarding War Diaries and Intelligence Summaries are contained in F. S. Regs., Part II. and the Staff Manual respectively. Title Pages will be prepared in manuscript.

WAR DIARY
or
~~INTELLIGENCE SUMMARY~~
(Erase heading not required.)

Army Form. C. 2118

Y/41 TRENCH MORTAR BATTERY

OCTOBER 1916

8

5,000 — Imp des A. C. — 24 7/15

Place	Date	Hour	Summary of Events and Information	Remarks and references to Appendices
ALBERT COMBINED SHEET 57d SE. 57c S.W. 62d NE. 62c NW	Oct 2		2/Lieut. J D. Bavin, R.F.A. posted from V/41 Trench Mortar Battery to command Y/41 Trench Mortar Battery. 2/Lieut. J D. Bavin took over the Battery, and found that 2/Lieut. R.W. Durno and part of personnel were forming part of Composite Battery at S.16 d 72 to be held in readiness to assist Infantry if required.	
S 6. c 77				
	Oct 2-31		Remainder of personnel assisting Field Batteries.	
S 16 d 72	Oct 9.		2/Lieut. J D. Bavin took over command of Composite Battery from Lieut. A. D. Overy and found that the majority of gunners had been sent to 183rd and 189th Brigades, R.F.A. for digging gun positions and dug-outs.	
	Oct 11		2/Lieut. J D. Bavin handed over the Composite Battery to Lieut. A.D. Overy and returned to Trench Mortar Headquarters at S. 6 c 77.	
	Oct 15.		Four guns, together with four guns of 30th Division prepared to go into action on left of GEUEDECOURT to destroy machine gun	

2

Instructions regarding War Diaries and Intelligence Summaries are contained in F. S. Regs., Part II. and the Staff Manual respectively. Title Pages will be prepared in manuscript.

WAR DIARY Y/41 Trench Mortar Battery
or
~~INTELLIGENCE SUMMARY~~
(Erase heading not required.)

OCTOBER 1916

Army Form. C. 2118

Place	Date	Hour	Summary of Events and Information	Remarks and references to Appendices
			emplacements which were hampering the advance of our Infantry. We were to use Gas Bombs. The 24 best men of the Composite Battery were selected and the guns taken into FLERS to be in readiness to move into the line. This Battery was to be commanded by Capt. J. A. H. Hill (the T.M.C.) with 2/Lieut. J. D. Bavin as second.	
	Oct 16		The only position within range of the target was reconnoitred and found to be a shallow trench not held by the Infantry during the day time. From this trench it was impossible to observe the target, and the position was found to be impracticable for Trench Mortars. The work of destroying the machine gun positions was eventually given to the 4.5 Howitzers. After dark the guns were brought back from FLERS.	
			Rounds fired. Nil.	
			Casualties. Died of wounds. 1 gunner.	

J. D. Bavin 2/Lieut. R.F.A.
O/C Y/41 Trench Mortar Battery

Instructions regarding War Diaries and Intelligence Summaries are contained in F. S. Regs., Part II. and the Staff Manual respectively. Title Pages will be prepared in manuscript.

WAR DIARY
or
INTELLIGENCE SUMMARY
(Erase heading not required.)

Army Form. C. 2118

Z/41 TRENCH MORTAR BATTERY

OCTOBER 1916

Place	Date	Hour	Summary of Events and Information	Remarks and references to Appendices
Nr Longueval	1/10/16 to 14/10/16		The personnel of Z Battery forming part of the composite advanced battery was employed on various fatigues with the Field Batteries of the Division & at the Dumps	
"	14/10/16	6.30 pm	Orders were received from the T.M.O. to recall all men of the Composite battery to take up the 4 guns etc to [illegible] & to select 25 N.C.O's men in readiness to proceed up the line in the morning.	
			The guns were therefore taken up & deposited at S.6.b.9.7 a guard being left in charge	
"	15/10/16		The personnel stood by until about 5 pm 15/10/16 when orders were received cancelling all arrangements, the guns being withdrawn to the old position near Longueval.	
"	16/10/16 to 31/10/16		During this period the personnel were again employed on various fatigues, training etc	
			Men of this battery not included in the composite battery were employed at T.M. H.Q. [illegible] during the whole period under review	

A. D. [illegible] Lt R.A. O.C. Z/41 T.M.B.

Army Form. C. 2118

Instructions regarding War Diaries and Intelligence Summaries are contained in F. S. Regs., Part II. and the Staff Manual respectively. Title Pages will be prepared in manuscript.

WAR DIARY HEADQUARTERS or ~~INTELLIGENCE SUMMARY~~ TRENCH. MORTAR BATTERIES 41 DIVISION

(Erase heading not required.)

OCTOBER 1916

5,000 — Imp. des A. C. — 24 7/15

Place	Date	Hour	Summary of Events and Information	Remarks and references to Appendices
S.16. d 72 (ALBERT) COMBINED SHEET 57 d S.E 57 c SW 62 d N.E. 62 c N.W	Oct 1-30		Composite Battery made up from X. Y. and Z. Batteries held in readiness to support Infantry.	
S. 6. c 77	Oct 1-30.		Trench Mortar Headquarters consisting of T.M.C and ration parties. The remainder of personnel were employed in assisting 18 pr. and 4.5 guns, and Ammunition Dump.	
	Oct 15.		Capt. G. Oakes o/c V/41. Trench Mortar Battery, attached to command D. Battery, 183rd Brigade R.F.A.	
	Oct 15.		Four guns together with four guns of 30th Division prepared to go into action on left of GEUEDECOURT to destroy machine gun emplacements which were hampering the advance of our Infantry. We were to use Gas Bombs. The 24 best men of the Composite Battery were selected and the guns taken to FLERS after dark to be in readiness to move into the line. This Battery was to be commanded by Capt. J. A. H. Hill (the T.M.C) with 2/Lieut. J. D. Barin as second.	

2/

OCTOBER 1916

Army Form. C. 2118

Instructions regarding War Diaries and Intelligence Summaries are contained in F. S. Regs., Part II. and the Staff Manual respectively. Title Pages will be prepared in manuscript.

WAR DIARY
or
~~INTELLIGENCE SUMMARY~~
(Erase heading not required.)

HEADQUARTERS TRENCH MORTAR BATTERIES 41 DIVISION

5,000 — Imp des A C — 24 7 15

Place	Date	Hour	Summary of Events and Information	Remarks and references to Appendices
	Oct 16		The only position within range of the target was reconnoitred and was found to be a shallow trench not held by the Infantry during the day time. From this trench it was impossible to observe the target, and the position was found impracticable for Trench Mortars. The work of destroying the machine gun positions was eventually given to the 4·5" Howitzers. After dark the guns were brought back from FLERS to S.16 d.72.	
	Oct 26		Capt J. A. H. Hill (the T.M.C) reported sick with Influenza, and was taken to the Field Ambulance by Motor. 2/Lieut. J D. Bavin took over of T.M.C	
	Oct 29.		Lieut. R. J. Harris returned from ~~temporary~~ permanent duty with C Battery, 189" Brigade R.F.A. to take over T.M.C.	
			Rounds fired Nil.	
			Casualties. Died of wounds. 2 gunners. Wounded. 1 gunner.	

J D Bavin 2/Lieut. R.F.A.
for T.M.C. 41 Division

Instructions regarding War Diaries and Intelligence Summaries are contained in F. S. Regs., Part II. and the Staff Manual respectively. Title pages will be prepared in manuscript.

WAR DIARY ~~or INTELLIGENCE SUMMARY~~. V/41 Trench Mortar Battery

(Erase heading not required.)

Army Form C. 2118.

November 1916

Place	Date	Hour	Summary of Events and Information	Remarks and references to Appendices
Mametz	31.10.16.	1 p.m.	Left for Le Neuville, where the Battery remained in rest.	
Le Neuville	8.11.16	6.0 am	Left for Morbecque, arrived 7 pm & billetted for the night	
Morbecque	9.11.16.	10.0 am	Left for Reninghelst, arrived 1.30 pm & occupied Victoria Camp.	
Reninghelst ~~Dickebusch~~	12.11.16	11.30 am	Left for permanent T.M. Billets near Dickebusch.	
Dickebusch	12.11.16.	6 pm	Took over positions, guns & stores from 4th Australian Division	
Do	13.11.16		Lieut Harris took over command of the Battery. vide D.A.R.O. No 64 13.11.16.	
Do	25.11.16		2nd Lieut. J.D. Bavin posted to take over command of Battery. vide D.A.R.O. No 123. 25.11.16.	

G.M. Jackson 2/Lt. R.F.A.

1

Instructions regarding War Diaries and Intelligence Summaries are contained in F. S. Regs., Part II. and the Staff Manual respectively. Title pages will be prepared in manuscript.

WAR DIARY X/41 TRENCH MORTAR BATTERY

or

~~INTELLIGENCE SUMMARY~~.

(Erase heading not required.)

Army Form C. 2118.

NOVEMBER 1916

Place	Date	Hour	Summary of Events and Information	Remarks and references to Appendices
Hametz	Oct. 31.		Moved by Lorries to Le Neuville, into Billets.	
Le Neuville	Nov. 8.		Leave Le Neuville by Lorries, arrive at Morbecque 7 pm. Billeted the night.	
Morbecque	Nov. 9.		Move on by Lorry; arrive Reninghelst 1 pm. All personel stay at Victoria Camp. B.C.'s and T.M.C. proceed to 4 Australian T.M. H.Q., near Dickebusch.	
Dickebusch	Nov. 12.		Took over from X 4 a. T.M.B. Exchanged 'Beds' & Guns only.	
	Nov. 15. to Nov. 30.		Daily firing with 1 Gun in Action. 30 rds. per diem. Wirecutting.	
	Nov. 16.		Pioneer Working Party commence work on 2 M.T.M. Emplacements in CANAL BANK.	
			Rounds Expended. 287	
			Casualties: NIL.	

G. Dilley. Lieut. R.F.A.
O.C. X/41 T.M.B.
30/11/16.

2353 Wt. W2544/1454 700,000 5/15 D. D. & L. A.D.S.S. Forms/C 2118.

Instructions regarding War Diaries and Intelligence Summaries are contained in F. S. Regs., Part II. and the Staff Manual respectively. Title pages will be prepared in manuscript.

WAR DIARY or ~~INTELLIGENCE SUMMARY~~. Y/41 TRENCH MORTAR BATTERY

Army Form C. 2118.

(Erase heading not required.)

NOVEMBER 1916

Place	Date	Hour	Summary of Events and Information	Remarks and references to Appendices
Mametz	Oct 31.		Moved by motor Lorries to Le Neuville, into billets.	
Le Neuville	Nov 8		Leave Le Neuville by motor Lorries, arrive at Morbecque 7 P.M. billet there for night	
Morbecque	Nov 9.		Move on by Motor Lorries, arrive Reninghelst 1 P.M. All personnel stay at Victoria Camp, Battery Commanders & T.M.O. go straight to 4 Australian T.M. Hd Qrs. near Dickebusch.	
Dickebusch	Nov ~~Oct~~ 12		Took over positions from Y/4 A. T.M. Batty. Exchanged "Beds" only.	
	Nov 18		Ordered to reconnoitre positions for T.M.s on 16 Dn. Front. for 41 Dn. Shoot, was only able to find positions for two guns.	
	Nov 19.		Party gets to work on positions on 16 Dn. front	
	Nov 22		Positions on 16 Dn. Front ready for action.	
	22, 23, 24, 25, 28, 29		Fire on enemy's support lines for half an hour each day. Enemy retaliates with 5.9s Heavy Minenwerfer, "Rum Jars" & "Fish Tails", but does no material damage.	
	Nov 25.		2/Lieut J. S. Bain R.F.A. posted to command V/41 T.M. Batty. 2/Lieut Dobson R.F.A. posted to command Y/41 T.M. Batty.	(DARO 123)
			Rounds Expended 132	
			Casualties - nil.	

J. S. Bain 2/Lt R.F.A.
for O/C Y/41 T.M. Batty

2353 Wt. W2544/1454 700,000 5/15 D. D. & L. A.D.S.S. Forms/C. 2118.

/ Instructions regarding War Diaries and Intelligence Summaries are contained in F. S. Regs., Part II. and the Staff Manual respectively. Title pages will be prepared in manuscript.

WAR DIARY Z/41 TRENCH MORTAR BATTERY

~~or~~

~~INTELLIGENCE SUMMARY.~~

(Erase heading not required.)

Army Form C. 2118.

NOVEMBER 1916

Place	Date	Hour	Summary of Events and Information	Remarks and references to Appendices
Mamely	31-10-16	1 pm	The battery together with others of the Brigade concentrated at ~~[illegible]~~ Mamely & left there by motor lorry for La Neuville	
La Neuville	1-11-16		~~[illegible]~~ The personnel was billeted at La Neuville until the 8-11-16 the period being spent in training & refitting	
Frohen	8-11-16	6 am	On the morning of the 8th inst the battery again proceeded by lorry to Frohen where it was billeted for the night	
Reninghelst	9-11-16		leaving the next morning for Reninghelst.	
Dickebusch	10-11-16		The battery remained at Reninghelst until the 10th inst when billets near Dickebusch were taken over from the 4th Australian T.M.B.	
St Eloi	12-11-16	10 am	The battery with two thirds of the personnel proceeded into the line taking over from Z/4 AUSTRALIAN battery an area of front stretching from O 2 c 5 6 to O 7 b 6 9 Wytschaete 1/10000 Sheet 28 S.W.2. The relief was completed by the evening of the 12th the officer from the Australian battery remaining in the line until the morning of the 13th	
St Eloi	13-11-16		The group commander inspected positions in the battery front	

Instructions regarding War Diaries and Intelligence Summaries are contained in F. S. Regs., Part II. and the Staff Manual respectively. Title pages will be prepared in manuscript.

WAR DIARY
or
INTELLIGENCE SUMMARY.
(Erase heading not required.)

Army Form C. 2118.

Place	Date	Hour	Summary of Events and Information	Remarks and references to Appendices
			O2.c q.6 & O2c.9.5½	
			Rds. Fired. 30. 4 Rds failed to explode on percussion.	
〃	18/11/16		Enemy's wire again fired upon at O2c. 9. 6½. Weather conditions bad. Wind caused erratic shooting & consequently results were only fair. Rds. Fired. 21. (2 Rds failed to explode on percussn)	
〃			Retaliation:– Several 5·9 inch shell fell in vicinity of O.1.d. 3 3.	
〃	19/11/16		Enemy's wire fired upon at O.2 c. 9½.8. Results again unsatisfactory owing to high & gusty wind. Retaliation. nil (on battery front). Rds fired 23. 2 Rds failed to explode	
〃	20/11/16		Enemy's wire at O.8. a 4.9½, to O 8 a 4.9¾ was fired on with good results. Rds. fired. 23.	
〃	21/11/16	2.15a.m	Crater O.2.c 9½ 6½. was fired upon from 2 emplacements. Results unobserved Retaliation. Heavy T.M. bombs & 7.7 cm shell on P.9 O. TRENCH.	
	21/11/16		Target O.8. a. 4½. 10. Results unobserved owing to weather conditions. Rds. fired. 21. (Boys-fuze) Retaliation negligible	

2353 Wt. W2544/1454 700,000 5/15 D. D. & L. A.D.S.S. Forms/C 2118.

Instructions regarding War Diaries and Intelligence Summaries are contained in F. S. Regs., Part II. and the Staff Manual respectively. Title pages will be prepared in manuscript.

WAR DIARY
or
INTELLIGENCE SUMMARY.
(Erase heading not required.)

Army Form C. 2118.

Place	Date	Hour	Summary of Events and Information	Remarks and references to Appendices
St. Eloi	22/11/16.	~~2.10pm~~	Operations. Nil.	
"	23/11/16	2.10pm to 2.40pm	Target. Enemy's wire 0.8.a.2½.8¼. Rds fired. 20. Results. Good. Retaliation. More than usual. Enemy shelled Bois Confluent with 7.7cm shell & trenches S. of P&O. Trench with Heavy T.M. bombs.	
"	24/11/16	~~3.5pm~~ 6" ~~3.35pm~~	Target. Enemy's wire O.2.c. 8½.5. Rds. fired 24. Results good, but shooting was erratic owing to wind. Retaliation. A few 5.9"cal shell fell in Bois Confluent, T.M. bombs. N.E. of CRATER LANE, & S. of P. & O. TRENCH.	
	25/11/16	3.5pm to 3.35pm	Target Enemy's wire 0.8.a 3½.9. Rds fired 6. Results good (Rifle mechanism jammed after 6 Rds., & could not be repaired before cessation of covering fire).	
	26/11/16	1.40pm to 2.10pm	Enemy's wire 0.2c 9.6½ was fired upon with 22 Rds. One Rd. failed to explode on percussion. Results only fair, owing to unstability of "bed" of gun, due to recent heavy rain. (Causing erratic shooting) Retaliation. A few T.M. bombs 300x N.E. of our area, a few 7.7.cm shell on communication trench E. of MOATED GRANGE (O.1.a.) & a large number of heavy T M bombs on S. side of P&O.TRENCH, some of which reached as far as SNIPERS BARN (O.1.c.)	[Retaliation considerably above normal today]

2353 Wt. W2544/1454 700,000 5/15 D. D. & L. A.D.S.S. Forms/C. 2118.

Army Form C. 2118.

Instructions regarding War Diaries and Intelligence Summaries are contained in F. S. Regs., Part II. and the Staff Manual respectively. Title pages will be prepared in manuscript.

WAR DIARY
or
INTELLIGENCE SUMMARY.

(Erase heading not required.)

Place	Date	Hour	Summary of Events and Information	Remarks and references to Appendices
St. Eloi	27/11/16		Operations. Nil. Arranged for 1 gun to be constantly in action ready to fire 10 Rds. in retaliation in event of any hostile T.M. bombs falling in our area.	
–	28/11/16	12.5 pm to 12.35 pm	Target. Enemy's front & support trenches round O.8.a.3.9. just N.E. of PICCADILLY FARM. Observation entirely impeded by a thick mist. Results unobserved. Rds. fired 20. Retaliation negligible.	
	29/11/16	1.30 pm to 2.0 pm	Target. Enemy's wire in front of trench running from O2c. 7½.5. to O2c. 9.5½. Rds. fired 25 Results good. Evidently enemy has a working party working on this portion of trench. One round fell in the trench & digging tools, duckboards & timber &c were observed to fly up in the air. Retaliation. 8 T.M. bombs on extreme left of our area as we were concluding our firing, & heavy T.M. bombs on trenches S. of P. & O. TRENCH	
–	30/11/16	12.0 noon to 12.30 pm	Target Enemy's wire in front of his front & support trenches round O.8a 4.9½. & O.8.a.5½.9½. 25 Rds were fired with good results. Enemy retaliated on BOIS CONFLUENT with 7.7 cm. shell at 12.15 pm, & later on trenches S. of P & O. TRENCH with heavy T.M. bombs.	
			Total Rds fired up to 30/11/16 . 262	
			Casualties. – – – – 1 (Slight & still at duty)	
			E. W. Raynor Sec. Lt. R.F.A. for O.C. Z/41. 30/11/16	

2353 Wt. W2544/1454 700,000 5/15 D. D. & L. A.D.S.S. Forms/C 2118.

Instructions regarding War Diaries and Intelligence Summaries are contained in F. S. Regs., Part II. and the Staff Manual respectively. Title Pages will be prepared in manuscript.

WAR DIARY

~~or~~

~~INTELLIGENCE SUMMARY~~

(Erase heading not required.)

DECEMBER. 1916

V/41 HEAVY TRENCH MORTAR BATTERY

Army Form C. 2118.

Place	Date	Hour	Summary of Events and Information	Remarks and references to Appendices
Dickebusch	1/12/16.		Have only one gun & one detachment in the line. Owing to faulty charges, & ~~have not yet~~ not having been able to obtain the new charges, we have not fired.	
"	31/12/16		Rounds fired. Nil.	
			Casualties. Nil.	
			J D Bavin 2/Lt RFA O/C V/41 T.M. Batty.	

2449 Wt. W14957/M90 750,000 1/16 J.B.C. & A. Forms/C.2118/12.

Instructions regarding War Diaries and Intelligence Summaries are contained in F. S. Regs., Part II. and the Staff Manual respectively. Title Pages will be prepared in manuscript.

WAR DIARY

~~or~~

~~INTELLIGENCE SUMMARY~~

(Erase heading not required.)

DECEMBER 1916

X/41 TRENCH MORTAR BATTERY

Army Form C. 2118.

Place	Date	Hour	Summary of Events and Information	Remarks and references to Appendices
Dickebusch	1/12/16	–	Remained in billets near Dickebusch & Battery was in action throughout the month in the ST. ELOI Sector.	
	1/12/16		1 Gun in Action – Wirecutting 0.2.d 1½. 6½. 32 rounds.	
	3/12/16		Night firing – Enemy's front line 0.4 a 3.4 – 0.4 a 4.4½. 65 rounds – 3 guns.	
	4/12/16		Daily Shoots discontinued. 'Duty' Gun for retaliation for enemy Minenwerfer fire starts firing.	
	16/12/16		2 Guns in Action – Front line 0.4 a 0.1 – 0.4 a 1.2. 40 rounds.	
	27/12/16		Test Shoots with Silencer by day & night. 33 rds. fired in all. 1 Premature round seriously wounded 2 of the gun team, both of whom died later.	
	31/12/16		1 Gun in Action – Wirecutting 0.4 a. 1½. 2½ – 0.4 a. 3.4. 30 rounds.	
			Casualties for month: 2 wounded (2 died)	
			Rounds fired: 247	
			31/12/16. G. Dilley. Lieut. R.F.A. O.C. X/41 T.M.B.	

2449 Wt. W14957/M90 750,000 1/16 J.B.C. & A. Forms/C.2118/12.

Instructions regarding War Diaries and Intelligence Summaries are contained in F. S. Regs., Part II. and the Staff Manual respectively. Title Pages will be prepared in manuscript.

1/

WAR DIARY

~~or~~

~~INTELLIGENCE SUMMARY~~

(Erase heading not required.)

DECEMBER 1916

Y/41 TRENCH MORTAR BATTERY

Army Form C. 2118.

Place	Date	Hour	Summary of Events and Information	Remarks and references to Appendices
DICKEBUSCH	Dec 1st		Took over command of Y.41 TMB from 2nd Lt. BAVIN.	
	Dec 2nd		Trench Raid - Fired 50 rounds on N18d 2.9½ N18b 1.1½ - 16th Div front	
	Dec 3rd		2 guns return from 16th Div front. Start work on offensive emplacements and bed for aeroplane shot on O13a 2.9½ and men's dugouts	
	Dec 10th	1.45 pm	Fired 48 rounds on front line O7b 33	
	Dec 14th	9.45 pm	The enemy raid front line trenches near CHICORY LANE - Fired 5 rounds from front line, but detachment driven away, and could not continue firing. Great damage done to two emplacements and front line by enemy.	
	Dec 20th		10 pioneers attached to Y.41 T.M.B - work on bombstores and defensive emplacements begun.	
	Dec 25th	10.45 am	Fired 40 rounds on O7b 44	
	Dec 27th	12 noon 8 pm	Fired rounds with silencer	
	Dec 30th	1.45 pm	Fired 45 rounds on Hostile T.M.s in BOIS QUARANTE under artillery support with excellent effect.	

Rounds expended ~~190~~ 234

Casualties - Nil -

H Dobson 2 Lt R.F.A
O.C. Y 41 TMB

2449 Wt. W14957/M90 750,000 1/16 J.B.C. & A. Forms/C.2118/12.

Instructions regarding War Diaries and Intelligence Summaries are contained in F. S. Regs., Part II. and the Staff Manual respectively. Title Pages will be prepared in manuscript.

WAR DIARY
~~or~~
~~INTELLIGENCE SUMMARY~~
(Erase heading not required.)

DECEMBER. 1916.

Z/41 TRENCH MORTAR BATTERY.

Army Form C. 2118.

Place	Date	Hour	Summary of Events and Information	Remarks and references to Appendices
ST. ELOI	1/xii/16	-9/xii/16	Work carried out in constructing new Offensive Positions	
– –	10/xii/16	3.30pm	10 Rounds fired by Retaliation Gun in accordance with scheme. Enemy commenced a bombardment of this Battery's front at 3.30p.m. using 7.7cm Shrapnel and 4.2" How, alongwith several T.M's. At 4.15pm all hostile shelling ceased.	
– –	11/xii/16 -	14/xii/16	Work continued on offensive emplacements, and four Defensive Emplacements commenced.	
– –	15/xii/16	9.30pm	4 rounds fired in accordance with Retaliation Scheme. Much Enemy activity, especially on Right.	
– –	16/xii/16 -	26/xii/16	Work continued on Offensive & Defensive Emplacements.	
– –	27/xii/16	12.25pm	Thirty Rounds fired (using Temple Silencer) on Enemy front line at O.8.a 9.3½. Results - fair - there being a large percentage of short rounds. Only a slow rate could be maintained. Enemy's activity was confined to about a dozen minenwerfer bombs.	'Silencer' found to be a failure for a shoot of this description.
– –	27/xii/16	8p.m	Two Rounds fired (using Temple Silencer) on enemy front line at O.8.a.9.3½. One failed to detonate. No further shooting possible on account of cordite being jammed. No Retaliation	
– –	28/xii/16 -	31/xii/16	Work continued in strengthening Emplacements & construction of new Defensive positions	
			Rounds fired. 46	
			Casualties Nil	

L. D. Rushbrooke Lieut R.F.A.
O/C Z/41 Trench Mortar Battery.

2449 Wt. W14957/M90 750,000 1/16 J.B.C. & A. Forms/C.2118/12.

Army Form C. 2118.

Instructions regarding War Diaries and Intelligence Summaries are contained in F. S. Regs., Part II. and the Staff Manual respectively. Title Pages will be prepared in manuscript.

WAR DIARY
or
INTELLIGENCE SUMMARY
(Erase heading not required.)

HEADQUARTERS
TRENCH MORTAR BATTERIES
41 DIVISION

Vol 10

Place	Date	Hour	Summary of Events and Information	Remarks and references to Appendices
DICKEBUSCH	DEC 1 to DEC 31 1916		Trench Mortar Billets and Headquarters at H. 31. d 8½. 1. No movement from Billets during month.	
			C. H. Oakes. Capt R.F.A. D.T.M.O. 41 Division	
			1.1.17.	

2449 Wt. W14957/M90 750,000 1/16 J.B.C. & A. Forms/C.2118/12.

Instructions regarding War Diaries and Intelligence Summaries are contained in F. S. Regs., Part II. and the Staff Manual respectively. Title Pages will be prepared in manuscript.

WAR DIARY
or
~~INTELLIGENCE SUMMARY~~
(Erase heading not required.)

Army Form C. 2118.

V/41 HEAVY TRENCH MORTAR BATTERY

JANUARY 1917

Place	Date	Hour	Summary of Events and Information	Remarks and references to Appendices
Dickebusch	1/1/17 to 16/1/17		Gun & Detachment in the line.	
	12/1/17		One Gun complete handed over to 47 Division	
	16/1/17		Two rounds fired with 17 oz charge at Target (Wytschaete 28 S.W.) O. 3 c. 8½. 4. First round fell from 15 to 20 yards in front of gun & failed to explode. Second round fell in No Mans Land. The Enemy then retaliated with ·77 cm 4·2's & 5·9"s two direct hits on pit with ·77 cm	
	23/1/17		Gun withdrawn from line for testing with "Dud" rounds.	
	31/1/17		Tests have not been carried out yet as material has been unobtainable	
	13/1/17		2 Lieut Marrians evacuated to England sick.	
			Rounds fired. Two	
			Casualties. Nil.	

Bavin
Lieut. R.F.A.
O/C V/41 T. M. Battery

2449 Wt. W14957/M90 750,000 1/16 J.B.C. & A. Forms/C.2118/12.

Army Form C. 2118.

Instructions regarding War Diaries and Intelligence Summaries are contained in F. S. Regs., Part II. and the Staff Manual respectively. Title Pages will be prepared in manuscript.

WAR DIARY ~~or~~ ~~INTELLIGENCE SUMMARY~~

(Erase heading not required.)

X/41 TRENCH MORTAR BATTERY

JANUARY 1917

Vol XI

Place	Date 1917	Hour	Summary of Events and Information	Remarks and references to Appendices
ST ELOI	Jan. 1. – 31.	–	Throughout the month, the Battery remained in action in the ST ELOI Sector. Many shoots were carried out, these chiefly comprising Wire-cutting. The wire was successfully cut for a Raid carried out by 11th Queens at about O. 3. d. 3.8.	
			Casualties: The only casualty throughout the month was one man slightly wounded whilst leaving the trenches.	
			Rounds fired: 416	
			Lieut. G. Dilley. R.F.A. performed the duties of D.T.M.O. vice Capt. G.H. Oakes R.F.A. (sick) from Jan. 1. – 21 incl. 2/Lieut. W.M. Pratt. R.F.A. during that period was in charge of X/41 T.M.B.	
			G. Dilley Lieut. R.F.A. O.C. X/41 T.M.B. 31/1/17	

2449 Wt. W14957/M90 750,000 1/16 J.B.C. & A. Forms/C.2118/12.

Y

Instructions regarding War Diaries and Intelligence Summaries are contained in F. S. Regs., Part II. and the Staff Manual respectively. Title Pages will be prepared in manuscript.

WAR DIARY
or
~~INTELLIGENCE SUMMARY~~

(Erase heading not required.)

Army Form C. 2118.

Y/41 TRENCH MORTAR BATTERY

JANUARY 1917

Place	Date	Hour	Summary of Events and Information	Remarks and references to Appendices
DIEPENDAAL	Jan 7th	2-4.30pm	Fired 65 rounds on wire N12d 2.0 – N12d 5.1½ – HOLLANDSCHESCHUUR REDOUBT	
	" 9th	a.m. 10-12.30pm	Fired 33 do do do Patrols report Wire badly damaged	
	"	"	Fired 54 rounds on wire O7b 2.2 – O7b 4.4 – BOIS QUARANTE with apparent good effect	
	"	7pm	Fired 66 rounds sweeping about O7d 4.9 / O7b 6½.1 } BOIS QUARANTE / N12d.8.0 HOLLANDSCHESCHUUR REDOUBT	"Dummy Raid"
	Jan 13th	3pm	Fired 5 rounds to keep wire open in O7b 4.4 BOIS QUARANTE	
	16th	3-4pm	Fired 57 rounds on wire O7b 4.4 – O7b 6.5 BOIS QUARANTE	
	18th	3.30-4pm	Fired 20 do do do do do Wire very badly damaged	
	19th	11.20pm	Fired 10 rounds onto O7b 6.1. in conjunction with 11th Queen's Raid	
	20th-30th		Work on damage done to emplacements by enemy; on removal of those "spotted" – building of bombstores, defensive emplacements – work much hindered by hard frost –	
	28th	–	6 D.A.C men attached to Battery	
	31st	2.30pm – 3.35pm	Fired rounds onto wire O7c 44 – O7c 4.9 – CROONAERT CAPEL	
			TOTAL ROUNDS FIRED 345 CASUALTIES – 1 N.C.O wounded / 2 men " / 1 N.C.O very slightly wounded	

H. D. Robinson [?] Lt RFA O.C. Y/41 T.M.B.

1/

Instructions regarding War Diaries and Intelligence Summaries are contained in F. S. Regs., Part II. and the Staff Manual respectively. Title Pages will be prepared in manuscript.

WAR DIARY
~~or~~
~~INTELLIGENCE SUMMARY~~
(Erase heading not required.)

Army Form C. 2118.

Z/41 TRENCH MORTAR BATTERY

JANUARY 1916

Place	Date	Hour	Summary of Events and Information	Remarks and references to Appendices
DICKEBUSCH.	Jan 1-5		Work continued on offensive + defensive emplacements	
"	" 6	2 p.m.	42 rounds fired on enemy wire from O 8 a 3½ 9½ to O 2 c 5½ 1. Exceptionally heavy retaliation.	As a result of this series of shoots the enemy's wire was completely destroyed at this part.
"	Jan 7.		As Jan 1-5.	
"	" 8	10 am	50 rounds fired on above target. Heavy retaliation.	
"	" 9.	–	59 rounds fired on above target, Piccadilly Farm. + enemy crater (O 2 c 9.5)	
"	" 10-13	–	As Jan. 1-5.	
"	" 14		15 rounds on above target. } Slight retaliation.	The guns of this battery are beginning to show signs of wear and there is a gas escape in consequence
"	" 15	3-5 pm	13 rounds on wire at O 2 c 5.1 }	
"	" 16.	2.20 pm	15 rounds on wire at O 2 c 5½. 1. }	
"	" 17	11.5 am	15 rounds on wire at O 2 c 5½. 1 Retaliation negligible	
"	" 18	10.20 am	10 rounds on wire at O 2 c 4½. 1. Little retaliation.	
"	" 19-23	—	As Jan 1-5	
"	" 23	11.30 am	8 rounds on enemy front line (registration of new emplacement)	
"	" 24-28	–	New dump for Z Bty completed, men's dug-outs strengthened, No. 8 offensive emplacement well in hand. Work all over severely handicapped for 2 week. by hard frost.	and 50 yards has to be added to the map ra.
"	" 29.	2 pm	33 rounds fired on Enemy wire from O 2 c 9½ 6½ to O 2 d. 1.7½. Slight retaliation. Results splendid. A practice "stand-to" in conjunction with infantry came off during the night	
"	" 30-31.	–	Work continued on No. 8. Defensive scheme arranged with infantry colonel – two guns to be brought into action in defensive positions in the event of foe attack + their occupation of our front line.	

Rounds expended. 260
Casualties NIL

Harold Thompson Lieut. R.F.A
o/c Z/41 TRENCH MORTAR BATTERY

2449 Wt. W14957/M90 750,000 1/16 J.B.C. & A. Forms/C.2118/12.

JANUARY 1917

Army Form C. 2118.

Instructions regarding War Diaries and Intelligence Summaries are contained in F. S. Regs., Part II. and the Staff Manual respectively. Title pages will be prepared in manuscript.

WAR DIARY or ~~INTELLIGENCE SUMMARY.~~

(Erase heading not required.)

HEADQUARTERS. TRENCH MORTAR BATTERIES 41 DIVISION

Place	Date	Hour	Summary of Events and Information	Remarks and references to Appendices
DICKEBUSCH	JAN. 1 To JAN. 31		Headquarters Trench Mortar Batteries, at H. 31 d. 8½ 1.	
			No movement from Headquarters during month.	
			C. H. Oakes. Capt R.F.A.	
			31. 1. 17 D.T.M.O. 41 Division	

2353 Wt. W2544/1454 700,000 5/15 D. D. & L. A.D.S.S./Forms/C. 2118.

Instructions regarding War Diaries and Intelligence Summaries are contained in F. S. Regs., Part II. and the Staff Manual respectively. Title pages will be prepared in manuscript.

WAR DIARY

~~or~~

~~INTELLIGENCE SUMMARY~~.

(*Erase heading not required.*)

FEBRUARY 1917

Army Form C. 2118.

V/41 HEAVY TRENCH MORTAR BATTERY

Place	Date	Hour	Summary of Events and Information	Remarks and references to Appendices
Dickebusch	1/2/17 to 10/2/17		Gun at rest billet for tests. Detachment only in the line to keep pumps going	
	10/2/17		Fired 6 "dud" rounds by billet to test gun found that the gun was shooting accurately & up to range.	
	11/2/17		Gun taken back into the line.	
	13/2/17		2/Lieut Hodson to C.C.S. sick.	
	16/2/17		2/Lieut. W. M. Pratt R.F.A. transferred to V/41 T.M. Batt. from X/41 T.M. Battery	
	21/2/17		Fired 3 rounds on Target map ref. sheet 28.S.W.2. O.3.d.4.2½. Retaliation heavy, but not near gun	
	23/2/17		Fired 9 rounds on Target sheet 28.S.W.2 map ref. O.3.d.8.3 do	
			Rounds fired 18.	
			Casualties Nil.	

H. D. Bowie.
Lieut. R.F.A.
O/C V/41. T.M. Battery

2353 Wt. W2544/1454 700,000 5/15 D. D. & L. A.D.S.S./Forms/C. 2118.

Instructions regarding War Diaries and Intelligence Summaries are contained in F. S. Regs., Part II. and the Staff Manual respectively. Title pages will be prepared in manuscript.

WAR DIARY

~~or~~

~~INTELLIGENCE SUMMARY~~.

(*Erase heading not required.*)

FEBRUARY 1917

X/41 TRENCH MORTAR BATTERY

Army Form C. 2118.

Place	Date	Hour	Summary of Events and Information	Remarks and references to Appendices
ST. ELOI	1917 Feb. 1-28	—	The Battery remained in action during this month in the St ELOI Sector, carrying out numerous wirecutting Shoots for Raids, etc. The wire was successfully cut for a night raid in O.4.a. on Feb. 8./17., about 500 rounds being fired in all. The Battery has not fired since that date, as all Rifle Mechanisms available were required for Y/41 T.M.B. Lieut. G. Dilley. R.F.A. took over D.T.M.O. from Feb. 17. – 28. 2/Lieut. A. Faller, 10th Queens, was attached to the Battery for duty from 5th Feb. 2/Lieut. W.M. Pratt R.F.A. was posted to V/41 H.T.M.B. on 17/2/17. Rounds fired during month: 405 Casualties (due to prematures): 7/Br. Filbee. } wounded. Gn. Randall. } Both evacuated from C.C.S. G. Dilley. Lieut. R.F.A. 28/2/17. O.C. X/41 T.M.B.	

2353 Wt. W2544/1454 700,000 5/15 D. D. & L. A.D.S.S./Forms/C. 2118.

Instructions regarding War Diaries and Intelligence Summaries are contained in F. S. Regs., Part II. and the Staff Manual respectively. Title pages will be prepared in manuscript.

WAR DIARY or ~~INTELLIGENCE SUMMARY~~.

(Erase heading not required.)

FEBRUARY 1917

Y/41 TRENCH MORTAR BATTERY

Army Form C. 2118.

Place	Date	Hour	Summary of Events and Information	Remarks and references to Appendices
WYTSCHAETE	1917 Feb. 1-28	–	The Battery remained in action in the Wytschaete Sector during the month, carrying out a lot of Shooting, chiefly wirecutting. The wire was cut for successful daylight raid carried out against the HOLLANDSCHAESCHUR SALIENT on Feb. 24./17. 1200 rounds were fired in connection with this task. A shoot with 6" Stokes Mortar was carried out with success on Feb. 24., 41 rounds being fired. Lieut. H. Dobbinson R.F.A. ceased to command battery on 16th Feb., being posted to Field Gun Battery. 2/Lieut. H. Thompson R.F.A. took over command of the Battery on the 26th Feb. Rounds fired during month:- 2" T.M. AMM. - 1388. 6" STOKES AMM. - 41 Casualties: 2/Lieut. R.W. Durno R.F.A. Killed in action 24/2/17. Bomb. G. Wright Killed by premature 18/2/17. Harold Thompson 2/Lieut. R.F.A. O.C. Y/41, T.M.B. 28/2/17.	

2353 Wt. W2544/1454 700,000 5/15 D. D. & L. A.D.S.S./Forms/C. 2118.

FEBRUARY 1917

Instructions regarding War Diaries and Intelligence Summaries are contained in F. S. Regs., Part II. and the Staff Manual respectively. Title pages will be prepared in manuscript.

WAR DIARY or ~~INTELLIGENCE SUMMARY.~~ Z/41 TRENCH MORTAR BATTERY

(Erase heading not required.)

Army Form C. 2118.

Place	Date	Hour	Summary of Events and Information	Remarks and references to Appendices
DICKEBUSCH	FEB 1	2-2.40 pm	101 rounds fired on enemy wire from 0.2 c 6½ 2 to 0.2 d 1.8. Result appeared to be very good. Normal retaliation.	
"	FEB 3	4-4.40 pm	60 rounds fired on enemy wire from 0 2 c 9½ 7 to 0 2 d 1.8 and at 0 2 c 6½ 2. Slight retaliation.	
"	FEB 6	2-2.40 pm	31 rounds fired on enemy wire from 0 2 c 9½ 7 to 0 2 d 1.8, and from 0 8 a 3 9 to 0.2 c 6½ 2. Normal retaliation.	
"	FEB 11	12 NOON 4 pm	13 rounds fired on enemy wire and front line trench at 0.7 c 4 4. Result very good. Slight retaliation	
"	FEB 20	3 pm 5 pm	48 rounds fired on enemy wire in front of crater area from 0.2 c to 0.2 d. Result very good. Retaliation Normal.	
"	FEB 21	2-2.45 pm	50 rounds fired on enemy wire in front of craters in 0.2 c and 0 2 d; also on machine gun emplacements and O.P.s at 0.2 c 5.2½ and 0.2 c 7 4. Result good. No retaliation.	
"	FEB 23	1 pm 1-45 pm	50 rounds fired on enemy wire in front of craters at 0 2 c & d. O.P. & new works 0 2 c 5.2½ and 0.2 c 7 4. Result Good. New works were damaged.	
			Casualties during month 1 N.C.O. and 1 Gunner wounded (1 slight). Rds fired 353	

A.J. [illegible] Lieut R.F.A.
O/C Z/41 TRENCH MORTAR BATTERY

T2134. Wt. W708–776. 500000. 4/15. Sir J. C. & S.

Instructions regarding War Diaries and Intelligence Summaries are contained in F. S. Regs., Part II. and the Staff Manual respectively. Title pages will be prepared in manuscript.

FEBRUARY 1917

Army Form C. 2118.

WAR DIARY
or
~~INTELLIGENCE SUMMARY.~~
(*Erase heading not required.*)

HEADQUARTERS
TRENCH MORTAR BATTERIES
41 DIVISION

Vol 12

Place	Date	Hour	Summary of Events and Information	Remarks and references to Appendices
DICKEBUSCH	FEB 1 To FEB 28		Headquarters Trench Mortar Batteries at H. 31 d 8½. 1.	
			No movement from Headquarters during month.	
			G. Willey Lieut R.F.A	
			28. 2. 17 D.T.M.O. 41 Division	

T2134. Wt. W708—776. 500000. 4/15. Sir J. C. & S.

1

Instructions regarding War Diaries and Intelligence Summaries are contained in F. S. Regs., Part II. and the Staff Manual respectively. Title pages will be prepared in manuscript.

WAR DIARY

~~or~~

~~INTELLIGENCE SUMMARY.~~

(Erase heading not required.)

MARCH 1917

V/41 HEAVY TRENCH MORTAR BATTERY

Army Form C. 2118.

Place	Date	Hour	Summary of Events and Information	Remarks and references to Appendices
Dickebusch	1/3/17 – 19/3/17		Gun and detachment in the line.	
	6/3/17		2/Lieut Hudson returned from C.C.S.	
	19/3/17		Ordered to take gun out of the line & to hand over to Motor Lorry waiting at Cafe Belge, gun handed over to Motor Lorry at 11.30 P.M. One Sergt & one gunner accompanied gun in lorry & obtained receipt from R.T.O Poperinge	
	23/3/17 – 24/3/17		Reconnoitred 5 positions for Heavy Mortars on Divl. Front	
	20/3/17 – 31/3/17		Detachment kept in the line to keep pit pumped out & stores clean.	
			Rounds fired Nil Casualties Nil.	

J.D. Brown
Capt. R.F.A.
O/C V/41 H.T.M. Batty

T2134. Wt. W708—776. 500000. 4/15. Sir J. C. & S.

1

Instructions regarding War Diaries and Intelligence Summaries are contained in F. S. Regs., Part II. and the Staff Manual respectively. Title pages will be prepared in manuscript.

WAR DIARY
or
~~INTELLIGENCE SUMMARY.~~
(Erase heading not required.)

MARCH 1917

X/41 TRENCH MORTAR BATTERY

Army Form C. 2118.

Place	Date	Hour	Summary of Events and Information	Remarks and references to Appendices
ST. ELOI.	1917 Mar. 1-31	–	The Battery remained in action at ST. ELOI during the month. Wirecutting (dud) was carried out on the Craters in O.2.d. during the first 10 days of the month. 'Steam-roller' wirecutting shoot carried out on night of 18/19 March with good results. 4 guns in action, 72 rounds fired in 20 minutes. Newton apple-iron beds in use for first time. A premature F occurred on 13/3/17, by which 2 Gunners were Killed, and one wounded. 2 Defensive Emplacements were completed during the month to fire on top of OLD KENT ROAD. 2 Defensive Emplacements commenced; to fire on ESTAMINET LANE. The foll. Officers ~~were~~ have been attached to the Battery during the month: 2/Lieut. C. Whitehouse R.F.A. and 2/Lieut. A.W. Pewtress R.F.A. 2/Lieut. A. Fuller attended course of one fortnight's duration at BERTHEN. Rounds fired during the month: 227 Casualties: As above. G. Tilley. Lieut. R.F.A. O.C. X/41 T.M.B. 31/3/17.	

Instructions regarding War Diaries and Intelligence Summaries are contained in F. S. Regs., Part II. and the Staff Manual respectively. Title pages will be prepared in manuscript.

WAR DIARY or ~~INTELLIGENCE SUMMARY~~.

(*Erase heading not required.*)

MARCH 1917

Y/41 TRENCH MORTAR BATTERY

Army Form C. 2118.

Place	Date	Hour	Summary of Events and Information	Remarks and references to Appendices
			This Battery was in action in the Diependaal Sector until the 24th of March, when it was relieved by X/16 T.M.B.	
			Only two shoots fall to be recorded. They were carried out on 7th & 8th March, on wire at O 7 c 3.8 and O 7 b 5.5, with successful results. As usual the retaliation was very heavy, but no casualties were sustained.	
			After the recent heavy shooting of this Battery it was found necessary to spend most time on checking and cleaning stores & ammunition.	
			The personnel of Y Bty is now attached to Z Bty to aid in the construction of new defensive & offensive emplacements.	
			Harold Thompson Lieut. for O.C. Y/41 T.M.B.	

T2134. Wt. W708—776. 500000. 4/15. Sir J. C. & S.

MARCH 1917

WAR DIARY
~~or~~
~~INTELLIGENCE SUMMARY~~.
(Erase heading not required.)

Z/41 TRENCH MORTAR BATTERY

Army Form C. 2118.

Instructions regarding War Diaries and Intelligence Summaries are contained in F. S. Regs., Part II. and the Staff Manual respectively. Title pages will be prepared in manuscript.

Place	Date	Hour	Summary of Events and Information	Remarks and references to Appendices
			During March this Battery remained in action on the left of the Diependaal Sector.	
			From 7th to 13th March heavy shooting was carried out on the enemy's wire about O 2 c (5-7)(1-3), preparatory to a raid over that ground. Three times the enemy came out & repaired the gaps caused by our shooting, but the wire was again opened. The retaliation was overwhelming, and considering the poor state & coverless nature of the trenches, the Battery made splendid practice. As a result Lieut Biddulph received the M.C., and three gunners the M.M. There were two men wounded during the operations.	
			The Battery shot with the 6" Stokes pattern gun on the 23rd inst. It was an experimental shoot & the results were good.	
			Two other shoots were made on enemy wire by night	
			Constructive work continues on the new offensive & defensive emplacements.	
			Harold Thompson Lieut for Lt O.C. Z Battery.	

T2134. Wt. W708—776. 500000. 4/15. Sir J. C. & S.

Instructions regarding War Diaries and Intelligence Summaries are contained in F. S. Regs., Part II. and the Staff Manual respectively. Title pages will be prepared in manuscript.

WAR DIARY
or
~~INTELLIGENCE SUMMARY.~~
(Erase heading not required.)

MARCH 1917

HEADQUARTERS
TRENCH MORTAR BATTERIES
41 DIVISION

Army Form C. 2118.

Vol 13

Place	Date	Hour	Summary of Events and Information	Remarks and references to Appendices
DICKEBUSCH	MCH 1 to MCH 31		HEADQUARTERS. TRENCH MORTAR BATTERIES. AT H. 31 d 8½. 1.	
			NO MOVEMENT FROM HEADQUARTERS DURING MONTH.	
			G. H. Oakes. CAPT. R.F.A.	
			31/3/17 D.T.M.O. 41 DIVISION	

Instructions regarding War Diaries and Intelligence Summaries are contained in F. S. Regs., Part II. and the Staff Manual respectively. Title pages will be prepared in manuscript.

WAR DIARY ~~or INTELLIGENCE SUMMARY.~~

(Erase heading not required.)

APRIL 1917

V/41 HEAVY TRENCH MORTAR BATTERY

Army Form C. 2118.

Place	Date	Hour	Summary of Events and Information	Remarks and references to Appendices
Dickebusch.	1/4/17 to 13/4/17		One detachment in the line, keeping Pit pumped out, ammunition clean and occupying dugouts.	
	13/4/17		Handed over Gun Pit, dugouts & 10 rounds ammunition complete to V/47 H T M Battery.	
	14/4/17 to 25/4/17		All personnel assisting Medium Trench Mortars build emplacements.	
	23/4/17		C. R. E. inspects the 5 proposed positions for Heavy Trench Mortars.	
	25/4/17		Start work digging 5 Heavy Mortar Emplacements under R. E. supervision at (Map. 28. S.W.2) O.1.a. 9 3/4. 3 1/2. (1 mortar), I.32. c. 9 3/4. 2. (2 mortars), and I.33. c. 5 1/2. 3. (2 mortars).	
			Rounds fired Nil.	
			Casualties Nil.	

J. H. Brown Capt. R.G.A.
O/C V/41 H. T. M Battery

Instructions regarding War Diaries and Intelligence Summaries are contained in F. S. Regs., Part II. and the Staff Manual respectively. Title pages will be prepared in manuscript.

WAR DIARY
~~or~~
~~INTELLIGENCE SUMMARY.~~
(Erase heading not required.)

APRIL 1917

X/41 TRENCH MORTAR BATTERY.

Army Form C. 2118.

Place	Date	Hour	Summary of Events and Information	Remarks and references to Appendices
St Eloi			This Battery was in action on the left front of the St Eloi front. On April 9th ~~[illegible]~~ the left part of our battery front was handed over to the 47th Division. On the 5th, 6th, 7th April operations were carried out. Target. Wire in front of Craters III & IV. Results were satisfactory. On the 27th evening operations were commenced. Target. Wire on Battery front. The time has chiefly been spent in building new emplacements to replace those handed over to the 47th Division & in renewing old positions.	

[illegible signature] Lt RFA.
OC X/41. T.M.B.

2353 Wt. W2544/1454 700,000 5/15 D. D. & L. A.D.S.S./Forms/C. 2118.

Instructions regarding War Diaries and Intelligence Summaries are contained in F. S. Regs., Part II. and the Staff Manual respectively. Title pages will be prepared in manuscript.

WAR DIARY

or

~~INTELLIGENCE SUMMARY.~~

(Erase heading not required.)

APRIL 1917

Y/41 TRENCH MORTAR BATTERY

Army Form C. 2118.

Place	Date	Hour	Summary of Events and Information	Remarks and references to Appendices
			During april this Battery has not been in action. They were assisting Z Battery in work of construction. Casualties - nil A E. Cundall 2 Lt O.C. Y/41. T.M.B.	

2353 Wt. W2544/1454 700,000 5/15 D. D. & L. A.D.S.S./Forms/C. 2118.

Instructions regarding War Diaries and Intelligence Summaries are contained in F. S. Regs., Part II. and the Staff Manual respectively. Title pages will be prepared in manuscript.

WAR DIARY
or
~~INTELLIGENCE SUMMARY.~~

(Erase heading not required.)

Z/41 TRENCH MORTAR BATTERY — APRIL 1917

Army Form C. 2118.

Place	Date	Hour	Summary of Events and Information	Remarks and references to Appendices
			During April this Battery remained in action in the St Eloi sector, and was frequently engaged on the task of wire-cutting. Shoots were carried out on the 4th, 5th, 6th & 7th; and on 24th, 25th, 27th, 28th, 29th & 30th. Altogether about 600 bombs were fired and the enemy's wire was kept in poor condition with numerous gaps. One casualty was sustained – Gr Priest being wounded in the back by our own 18 pr. fire. On the 27th the enemy left his front line trenches at the opening of our bombardment and ran across the open for the reserve line. This is very unusual. Covering fire from the Artillery has been excellent and retaliation slighter than heretofore. There are fewer hostile T.Ms on this front than during March.	
			With the assistance of half of Y Battery work of construction was carried out on several new offensive pits, which are now practically completed.	
			Harold Thompson. Lieut. O.C. Z/41 T.M.B.	

2353 Wt. W2544/1454 700,000 5/15 D. D. & L. A.D.S.S./Forms/C. 2118.

APRIL 1917

Army Form C. 2118.

Instructions regarding War Diaries and Intelligence Summaries are contained in F. S. Regs., Part II. and the Staff Manual respectively. Title pages will be prepared in manuscript.

WAR DIARY
or
~~INTELLIGENCE SUMMARY.~~

HEADQUARTERS. TRENCH MORTAR BATTERIES 41 DIVISION

(Erase heading not required.)

Vol 14

Place	Date	Hour	Summary of Events and Information	Remarks and references to Appendices
DICKEBUSCH	APR. 1 to APR. 30		HEADQUARTERS TRENCH MORTAR BATTERIES AT H. 31. d 8½. 1.	
			NO MOVEMENT FROM HEADQUARTERS DURING MONTH.	
			C. H. Oakes. CAPT. R.F.A.	
			30/4/17 D.T.M.O. 41 DIVISION	

2353 Wt. W2544/1454 700,000 5/15 D. D. & L. A.D.S.S./Forms/C. 2118.

Instructions regarding War Diaries and Intelligence Summaries are contained in F. S. Regs., Par. II. and the Staff Manual respectively. Title pages will be prepared in manuscript.

WAR DIARY

or

~~INTELLIGENCE SUMMARY.~~

(*Erase heading not required.*)

MAY 1917

Army Form C. 2118.

V/41 HEAVY TRENCH MORTAR BATTERY

Place	Date	Hour	Summary of Events and Information	Remarks and references to Appendices
Dickebusch	1/5/17 } 31/5/17 }.		Working on 8 Heavy Trench Mortar Emplacements under R.E. Supervision.	
	8/5/17.		2 Lieut Pope R.F.A. attached to V/41 HTM Battery for duty.	
			Rounds fired: Nil Casualties Nil.	
			[signature] Capt. RFA. O/C V/41 HTM Battery	

A6945 Wt. W11422/M1160 350,000 12/16 D. D. & L. Forms/C./2118/14.

Instructions regarding War Diaries and Intelligence Summaries are contained in F. S. Regs., Par. II. and the Staff Manual respectively. Title pages will be prepared in manuscript.

WAR DIARY ~~or INTELLIGENCE SUMMARY~~.

(*Erase heading not required.*)

MAY/1917

X/41 TRENCH MORTAR BATTERY

Army Form C. 2118.

Place	Date	Hour	Summary of Events and Information	Remarks and references to Appendices
St Eloi			The Battery was in action the whole of the month in the St Eloi Sector & covered the left front of this sector. On the 1st of May on the promotion of Lieut Lilley to D.T.M.O. 2Lt AW Pestress assumed command of the battery from that date.	
			Wirecutting was commenced on May 13th & continued up to the end of the month an average of 50 rds per day being fired (700 Rds). Extent of target being O3b 50.00 to O2d 5070. The result was satisfactory from O2d 50.70 to O3c 7050. The wire on the east of these points not being engaged.	
			Work was carried out during the month on existing emplacements & seven new positions were built.	
			One casualty was suffered during the month 122669 Gr G Hewitt being wounded on the 29th in Voormezeele.	
			2Lieut Harris was attached to the Battery for duty on the 24th.	

AW Pestress
Lt RFA
OC X.41

A6945 Wt. W11422/M1160 350,000 12/16 D. D. & L. Forms/C./2118/14.

Instructions regarding War Diaries and Intelligence Summaries are contained in F. S. Regs., Par. II, and the Staff Manual respectively. Title pages will be prepared in manuscript.

WAR DIARY

or

~~INTELLIGENCE SUMMARY~~.

(*Erase heading not required.*)

Army Form C. 2118.

MAY 1917

Y/41 TRENCH MORTAR BATTERY

Place	Date	Hour	Summary of Events and Information	Remarks and references to Appendices
			During May this Battery has not been in action.	
			The personnel were assisting X Battery in constructional work	
			Casualties Nil	
			W Parker 2Lt	
			for OC Y/41	
			T.17.B.	

A6945 Wt. W11422/M1160 350,000 12/16 D. D. & L. Forms/C./2118/14.

Instructions regarding War Diaries and Intelligence Summaries are contained in F. S. Regs., Par. II, and the Staff Manual respectively. Title pages will be prepared in manuscript.

Army Form C. 2118.

WAR DIARY

~~or~~

~~INTELLIGENCE SUMMARY.~~ Z/41 TRENCH MORTAR BATTERY

(Erase heading not required.)

MAY. 1917

Place	Date	Hour	Summary of Events and Information	Remarks and references to Appendices
ST. ELOI	MAY.	—	During May this Battery remained in action in the St. Eloi Sector, and completed the task of wire-cutting along its entire front. Series of shoots were carried out on three occasions, involving an expenditure of about 750 bombs. The wire up to the foe support line was shattered and kept cut. By arrangement with the Infantry holding the line, a sharp look-out was kept lest the enemy should re-wire, and he suffered casualties in the attempt. No casualties were sustained by this battery during the month. The retaliation was slight, the T.M's that were so much in evidence during our winter shoots apparently having been removed. Several gunpits were however blown up by shellfire. Constructive work on new offensive pits was brought to completion this month, & five pits handed over to Z/1 TMB on the 30th for their exclusive use.	
			Harold Thompson, Lieut R.F.A. O.C. Z/41 TMB.	

A6945 Wt. W11422/M1160 350,000 12/16 D. D. & L. Forms/C./2118/14.

MAY 1917

Army Form C. 2118.

Instructions regarding War Diaries and Intelligence Summaries are contained in F. S. Regs., Part II. and the Staff Manual respectively. Title pages will be prepared in manuscript.

WAR DIARY ~~or~~ ~~INTELLIGENCE SUMMARY~~.

HEADQUARTERS TRENCH MORTAR BATTERIES 41 DIVISION

(*Erase heading not required.*)

Vol 15

Place	Date	Hour	Summary of Events and Information	Remarks and references to Appendices
DICKEBUSCH	MAY 1		HEADQUARTERS TRENCH MORTAR BATTERIES AT H 31 d 8½ 1.	
	To			
	MAY 31		NO MOVEMENT FROM HEADQUARTERS DURING MONTH	
			G. Tilley CAPT. R.F.A	
			D.T.M.O. 41 DIVISION	

A6945 Wt. W11422/M1160 350,000 12/16 D. D. & L. Forms/C./2118/14.

JUNE 1917

Army Form C. 2118.

Instructions regarding War Diaries and Intelligence Summaries are contained in F. S. Regs., Part II, and the Staff Manual respectively. Title pages will be prepared in manuscript.

WAR DIARY
or
~~INTELLIGENCE~~ SUMMARY.
(Erase heading not required.)

V/41
HEAVY TRENCH MORTAR BATTERY

Place	Date	Hour	Summary of Events and Information	Remarks and references to Appendices
Dickebusch.	1-2.		Getting up guns & ammunition to emplacements.	
	2.		Handed over 1. 9.45 H.T.M. in action to V/1 H.T.M. Battery.	
	3 4 5 6		Firing in preliminary bombardment for offensive. Guns in action 3.	
	7.		1 officer & 16 ORs searching for captured guns. found three 77 cms field guns, impossible to remove at time.	
	8-10		Removing guns & stores from emplacements, salving material used & collecting ammunition.	
	13.		Started digging emplacement for new improved long range 9.45 HTM	
	13-30		Building emplacement, & getting everything ready for action	
			Rounds fired 167.	
			Casualties: 4 ORs wounded.	

[signature] Capt. RGA
O/c V/41 HTM Battery

A6945 Wt. W11422/M1160 350,000 12/16 D. D. & L. Forms/C./2118/14.

Instructions regarding War Diaries and Intelligence Summaries are contained in F. S. Regs., Part II. and the Staff Manual respectively. Title pages will be prepared in manuscript.

JUNE 1917

WAR DIARY

~~or INTELLIGENCE~~ SUMMARY.

(*Erase heading not required.*)

X/41 TRENCH MORTAR BATTERY

Army Form C. 2118.

Place	Date	Hour	Summary of Events and Information	Remarks and references to Appendices
			The Battery was in action in the St Eloi sector & covered the left front of it.	
			Wirecutting was carried out up to June 6th daily an average of 150 Rds being fired each day.	
			The battery was reinforced by X/1 who also fired the same number of rds having 5 guns in action making a total of 9 guns on our front.	
			Sgt H.W. Lea of Y battery & Corpl W Smith of X battery were wounded by a premature on June 6th.	
			After June 7th the battery came out of action after clearing up the Ammunition & emplacements & did not come into action again during the month.	
			H W Pewtress Lt. RFA. OC X.41 T.M.B.	

A6945 Wt. W11422/M1160 350,000 12/16 D. D. & L. Forms/C./2118/14.

JUNE 1917

Army Form C. 2118.

Instructions regarding War Diaries and Intelligence Summaries are contained in F. S. Regs., Par. II. and the Staff Manual respectively. Title pages will be prepared in manuscript.

WAR DIARY 2/41

or

~~INTELLIGENCE SUMMARY~~. TRENCH MORTAR BATTERY

(*Erase heading not required.*)

Place	Date	Hour	Summary of Events and Information	Remarks and references to Appendices
ST. ELOI			During the first week of this month this battery, assisted by one-half of Y/41 T.M.B., took part in the preliminary bombardment, having previously cut all the wire on its front. 841 rounds were fired. Since June 7th work continued in the line in demolishing gun pits after the advance, & in salving ammunition. Otherwise there is nothing to report.	
			Two casualties were sustained on June 4th:-	
			1. 102334 Gr. Smart, Z/41, killed by premature.	
			1. 1321 Gr. Northover, Z/41, wounded by do.	
			Harold Thompson. Lieut. R.F.A. O.C. Z/41 T.M.B.	

A6945 Wt. W11422/M1160 350,000 12/16 D. D. & L. Forms/C./2118/14.

JUNE 1917

Army Form C. 2118.

Instructions regarding War Diaries and Intelligence Summaries are contained in F. S. Regs., Part II. and the Staff Manual respectively. Title pages will be prepared in manuscript.

WAR DIARY
or
~~INTELLIGENCE~~ SUMMARY.
(Erase heading not required.)

Y/41 TRENCH MORTAR BATTERY

Place	Date	Hour	Summary of Events and Information	Remarks and references to Appendices
St Eloi	30/6/17		During the month of June this battery has not been in action. The personnel were assisting X & Z batteries	
			Casualties. 1 Sergt wounded.	
			A E Cundall Lt O/c Y/41 TMB	

A6945 Wt. W11422/M1160 350,000 12/16 D. D. & L. Forms/C./2118/14.

JUNE 1917

Instructions regarding War Diaries and Intelligence Summaries are contained in F. S. Regs., Par. II. and the Staff Manual respectively. Title pages will be prepared in manuscript.

WAR DIARY

~~or~~

~~INTELLIGENCE SUMMARY.~~

(*Erase heading not required.*)

HEADQUARTERS TRENCH MORTAR BATTERIES. 41 DIVISION.

Army Form C. 2118.

Vol 16

Place	Date	Hour	Summary of Events and Information	Remarks and references to Appendices
DICKEBUSCH	JUNE 1		HEADQUARTERS TRENCH MORTAR BATTERIES AT H 31 d 8½ 1.	
	TO			
	JUNE 30		NO MOVEMENT FROM HEADQUARTERS DURING MONTH.	
			G. Tilley. CAPT. R.F.A.	
			30/6/17 D.T.M.O. 41 DIVISION	

A6945 Wt. W11422/M1160 350,000 12/16 D. D. & L. Forms/C./2118/14.

Army Form C. 2118.

Instructions regarding War Diaries and Intelligence Summaries are contained in F. S. Regs., Part II. and the Staff Manual respectively. Title pages will be prepared in manuscript.

WAR DIARY
or
~~INTELLIGENCE SUMMARY.~~
(Erase heading not required.)

JULY 1917

V/41 TRENCH MORTAR BATTERY

Place	Date	Hour	Summary of Events and Information	Remarks and references to Appendices
Dickebusch	July 1 to 4		On emplacement for New Long Range 9.45 Mk II Mortar	
	5		Handed over to V/47 H.T.M. Battery, & go to Divl Rest near Boeschepe	
Boeschepe	12.		2 Lieut G. M. Hudson R.G.A. transferred to "H" Battery Anti Aircraft.	
	19		2 Lieut. Pope R.G.A. posted to V/41 H.T.M. Battery	
Dickebusch	23		Returned to line and took over from V/47 H.T.M. Battery	
	24 to 29		Personnel on fatigues for Field Batteries, and Medium T.M. Batteries	
			Rounds fired: Nil	
			Casualties: 1 gunner Killed 3 gunners Gassed	

J. Bavin
Capt. R.G.A.
O/C V/41 H.T.M. Battery

2353 Wt. W2544/1454 700,000 5/15 D. D. & L. A.D.S.S./Forms/C. 2118.

Army Form C. 2118.

Instructions regarding War Diaries and Intelligence Summaries are contained in F. S. Regs., Part II. and the Staff Manual respectively. Title pages will be prepared in manuscript.

WAR DIARY
or
~~INTELLIGENCE SUMMARY.~~

(*Erase heading not required.*)

JULY 1917

X/41 TRENCH MORTAR BATTERY

Place	Date	Hour	Summary of Events and Information	Remarks and references to Appendices
			The Battery was not in action this month except on the 29th when 240 Rds were fired from the new 6" Newton Mortars. On July 5th the battery went to the rest & returned on the 23rd. most of which time was spent in digging emplacements for field batteries.	
			Casualties: 1 N C O and gunner wounded 1 gunner gassed	
			2Lt. Fuller was transferred to Z battery & 2Lt. Lord took his place.	

[illegible] Lt. RFA
OC X 41 T.M.B.

2353 Wt. W2544/1454 700,000 5/15 D. D. & L. A.D.S.S./Forms/C. 2118.

Instructions regarding War Diaries and Intelligence Summaries are contained in F. S. Regs., Part II. and the Staff Manual respectively. Title pages will be prepared in manuscript.

WAR DIARY

~~or~~

~~INTELLIGENCE SUMMARY.~~

(*Erase heading not required.*)

Army Form C. 2118.

JULY 1917

Y/41

TRENCH MORTAR BATTERY

Place	Date	Hour	Summary of Events and Information	Remarks and references to Appendices
			This Battery was only in action this month on the 29th + 30th inst when 202 rounds were fired from the new 6" Newton Mortar. The personnel were in rest from the 5th till the 23rd inst. Fatigues for field batteries occupied most days.	
			Casualties:- 1 gunner wounded 3 gunners gassed (1 since died)	
			2nd Lt R. M. Marians ~~tat~~ attached to this battery on the 31st inst	
			A. E. Cundall Lt RFA Y/41 T.M.B	

2353 Wt. W2544/1454 700,000 5/15 D. D. & L. A.D.S.S./Forms/C. 2118.

JULY 1917

Army Form C. 2118.

Instructions regarding War Diaries and Intelligence Summaries are contained in F. S. Regs., Part II. and the Staff Manual respectively. Title pages will be prepared in manuscript.

WAR DIARY

~~or~~

~~INTELLIGENCE SUMMARY.~~

(Erase heading not required.)

Z/41 TRENCH MORTAR BATTERY

Place	Date	Hour	Summary of Events and Information	Remarks and references to Appendices
			This Battery was in action on the 29th of this month, when they assisted Z & Y batteries to fire the new 6" Newton Mortars.	
			The Battery went out to rest from the 5th until the 23rd inst, — the remainder of the month was mostly spent in fatigues for field batteries.	
			Casualties:— 2 N.C.O's and 1 gunner wounded	
			2 N.C.O's and 7 gunners gassed (3 gunners since died)	
			Lieut H. Thompson O.C of this battery was transferred on the 25th inst to an Anti-Aircraft Battery his place being taken by 2Lt A. Faller.	
			2Lt G. J. Lamb was transferred from this battery to X battery dated 25th inst —	
			A. Faller 2Lt R.F.A	
			Z/41 T.M.B.	

2353 Wt. W2544/1454 700,000 5/15 D. D. & L. A.D.S.S./Forms/C. 2118.

Instructions regarding War Diaries and Intelligence Summaries are contained in F. S. Regs., Part II. and the Staff Manual respectively. Title pages will be prepared in manuscript.

WAR DIARY

~~or~~

~~INTELLIGENCE SUMMARY.~~

(*Erase heading not required.*)

JULY 1917

Army Form C. 2118.

HEADQUARTERS TRENCH MORTAR BATTERIES 41 DIVISION.

Vol 1

Place	Date	Hour	Summary of Events and Information	Remarks and references to Appendices
DICKEBUSCH. H 31 d 8½ 1	JULY 1-5		HEADQUARTERS TRENCH MORTAR BATTERIES 41 DIVISION	
BOESCHEPE R 15 a 0.3	JULY 5-23		MOVED INTO REST BILLETS.	
DICKEBUSCH N 1 b 2.5	JULY 23-31		RETURNED FROM REST BILLETS.	
			C. Tilley CAPT. R.F.A	
			31/7/17 D.T.M.O. 41 DIVISION	

2353 Wt. W2544/1454 700,000 5/15 D. D. & L. A.D.S.S./Forms/C. 2118.

Instructions regarding War Diaries and Intelligence Summaries are contained in F. S. Regs., Part II. and the Staff Manual respectively. Title pages will be prepared in manuscript.

WAR DIARY
or
~~INTELLIGENCE SUMMARY~~.
(*Erase heading not required.*)

AUGUST 1917

V/41 TRENCH MORTAR BATTERY

Army Form C. 2118.

Place	Date	Hour	Summary of Events and Information	Remarks and references to Appendices
Dickebusch	1 Aug to 13 Aug		Constructing emplacement for Mk II Long 9.45 T.M.	
	14 Aug.		Fired 20 rounds on Locks 5 to south (Map 28 S.W.2.) O. 12. b. 85. 40.	
	19 Aug.		" 20 rounds on Canal & Railway Bank. O.6. c. 98. 05 to O.12. b. 20. 90	Sheet 28. S.W. 2.
	20 Aug to 27 Aug		Constructing new emplacement for Mortar. Long 9.45 Mk II.	
	28 Aug		Fired 15 rounds at Coy Hd Qrs. J. 31. d. 45. 44. and shell-hole dugouts J. 31 c. 70. 60.	
	30 Aug.		" 9 rounds at O.6. d. 05. 95. P. 7. a 15. 77. O. 12 b. 45. 45	
			Rounds fired. 64	
			Casualties. 2 N. C.O's and 1 gunner wounded	

J. H. Barlin
Capt. R.F.A.
O/c V/41 T.M. Battery

Instructions regarding War Diaries and Intelligence Summaries are contained in F. S. Regs., Part II. and the Staff Manual respectively. Title pages will be prepared in manuscript.

AUGUST 1917

WAR DIARY
~~or~~
~~INTELLIGENCE SUMMARY.~~
(Erase heading not required.)

X/41 TRENCH MORTAR BATTERY. Army Form C. 2118.

Place	Date	Hour	Summary of Events and Information	Remarks and references to Appendices
			This battery was not in action as a separate unit during the month. The 2" Mortars were not used at all. The new 6" Mortars (4 in number) was fired for the purpose of cutting wire & destroying trenches & proved satisfactory. The personnel of the battery were used in carrying ammunition for the H.T.M. Battery & were also used for general fatigues. Casualties. Nil A W Pewtress Lt. RFA OC X 41 TMB.	

T2134. Wt. W708—776. 500000. 4/15. Sir J. C. & S.

Instructions regarding War Diaries and Intelligence Summaries are contained in F. S. Regs., Part II. and the Staff Manual respectively. Title pages will be prepared in manuscript.

WAR DIARY ~~or INTELLIGENCE SUMMARY.~~ Y/41 TRENCH MORTAR BATTERY

(*Erase heading not required.*)

AUGUST 1917

Army Form C. 2118.

Place	Date	Hour	Summary of Events and Information	Remarks and references to Appendices
	31/8/17		Participated in 6" Shoots on Aug 17th and 27th. Ammunition fatigues for Heavy Battery and Instruction and Drill in 6" Mortar occupied remainder of month.	
			Casualties Nil	
			A. E. Cundall Lt R.F.A. O/c Y/41 T.M.B.	

T2134. Wt. W708—776. 500000. 4/15. Sir J. C. & S.

Instructions regarding War Diaries and Intelligence Summaries are contained in F. S. Regs., Part II. and the Staff Manual respectively. Title pages will be prepared in manuscript.

AUGUST 1917

WAR DIARY or ~~INTELLIGENCE SUMMARY~~. Z/41 TRENCH MORTAR BATTERY.

(*Erase heading not required.*)

Army Form C. 2118.

Place	Date	Hour	Summary of Events and Information	Remarks and references to Appendices
31/8/17.			This battery was not in action as a separate unit during the month. The 2" mortar was not used at all. The new 6" Newton mortars (four in number) were fired for the purpose of cutting wire & destroying trenches & strong points, & proved very satisfactory The personnel of the battery were used in carrying ammunition for the Heavy Trench Mortar Battery & were also used for general fatigues Casualties nil. [signature] 2nd Lieut RFA for O/C Z/41 M.T.M.B.	

T2134. Wt. W708–776. 500000. 4/15. Sir J. C. & S.

AUGUST 1917

Army Form C. 2118.

Instructions regarding War Diaries and Intelligence Summaries are contained in F. S. Regs., Part II. and the Staff Manual respectively. Title pages will be prepared in manuscript.

WAR DIARY

or

~~INTELLIGENCE SUMMARY.~~

(*Erase heading not required.*)

HEADQUARTERS TRENCH MORTAR BATTERIES 41 DIVISION

Vol 18

Place	Date	Hour	Summary of Events and Information	Remarks and references to Appendices
DICKEBUSCH	AUG 1		HEADQUARTERS, TRENCH MORTAR BATTERIES. 41 DIVISION.	
N 1. b 2.5.	AUG. 31.			
			NO MOVEMENT FROM BILLET DURING THE MONTH.	
			31/8/17	
			G. Tilley. CAPT. R. F. A. D.T.M.O., 41st Division	

T2134. Wt. W708–776. 500000. 4/15. Sir J. C. & S.

Army Form. C. 2118

Instructions regarding War Diaries and Intelligence Summaries are contained in F. S. Regs., Part II. and the Staff Manual respectively. Title Pages will be prepared in manuscript.

WAR DIARY
or
~~INTELLIGENCE SUMMARY~~
(Erase heading not required.)

SEPTEMBER 1917

V/41 HEAVY "TRENCH" MORTAR BATTERY

5,000 — Imp. des A. C. — 24.7.15

Place	Date	Hour	Summary of Events and Information	Remarks and references to Appendices
Dickebusch	Sept 1.		Handed over to V/39 H.T.M. Battery. 2 Mk II Improved 9.45 T.Ms. in action. 3 Mk I 9.45 T.Ms. at Billet.	
"	2		Moved to rest in Boeschepe Area.	
"	12		Returned from Boeschepe Area to line	
"	13 to 30		Personnel on fatigues for Field Batteries and R.Es	
			Rounds fired. Nil.	
			Casualties. A. 141345 Gnr E. Rice wounded 24.9.17	
			A. 127213 Gnr G. Pocock wounded 28.9.17	
			[signature] Capt R.F.A. O/C V/41 HTM Battery	

Instructions regarding War Diaries and Intelligence Summaries are contained in F. S. Regs., Part II. and the Staff Manual respectively. Title Pages will be prepared in manuscript.

WAR DIARY
~~or~~
~~INTELLIGENCE SUMMARY~~
(Erase heading not required.)

SEPTEMBER 1917

X/41 TRENCH MORTAR BATTERY

Army Form. C. 2118

Place	Date	Hour	Summary of Events and Information	Remarks and references to Appendices
			This battery went out to rest in the Boeschepe area on the 2nd & returned to the line on the 12th. One 6" Newton T. M. was put in the line in Shrewsbury Forest to knock out some wire. 100 rds were fired at this target on the 17th & the gun was put out of action by a shell on the 18th. No more firing was undertaken. All the men were taken up for fatigues for the field batteries for the remainder of the month.	
			Casualties. No 33382 Davison J. Cpl. wounded 25/9/17	
			No 40980 Saunders A. J. Dr. " 25/9/17	
			No 28053 Mactel G. H. Sgt. died of wounds 28/9/17	
			H W Pewtress Lt. RFA OC. X 41 T.M.B.	

Army Form. C. 2118

Instructions regarding War Diaries and Intelligence Summaries are contained in F. S. Regs., Part II. and the Staff Manual respectively. Title Pages will be prepared in manuscript.

WAR DIARY

or

~~INTELLIGENCE SUMMARY~~

(Erase heading not required.)

SEPTEMBER 1917

Y/41 TRENCH. MORTAR BATTERY

3.050 – Imp des A C – 24 7/15

Place	Date	Hour	Summary of Events and Information	Remarks and references to Appendices
			This battery went out to rest in the Boeschepe area on the 2nd inst & returned to the line on the 12th. Fatigues for Field Batteries occupied the remainder of the month. No T M shoots were undertaken by this battery	
			Casualties:-	
			M. 28794 Gnr Sheffield. H. wounded 28/9/17	
			M. 40496 Gnr J. Stamper wounded 28/9/17.	
			A. E. Cundall Lt RFA O/c Y/41 T.M.B	

Instructions regarding War Diaries and Intelligence Summaries are contained in F. S. Regs., Part II. and the Staff Manual respectively. Title Pages will be prepared in manuscript.

WAR DIARY

or

~~INTELLIGENCE SUMMARY~~ Z/41 TRENCH MORTAR BATTERY

(Erase heading not required.)

SEPTEMBER 1917

Army Form. C. 2118

Place	Date	Hour	Summary of Events and Information	Remarks and references to Appendices
			This battery has not been in action as a separate unit during the current month. Personnel of the battery have been employed on fatigues, relieving gunners of 190th Bde R.F.A. & assisting in road making. Casualties Killed 38454 Cpl Maine V. 196283 Gnr Taylor H. Wounded 168858 Dvr Leonard [signature] Lieut R.F.A. O/C Z/41 M.T.M.B.	

Army Form. C. 2118

WAR DIARY
or
~~INTELLIGENCE SUMMARY~~
(Erase heading not required.)

SEPTEMBER 1917
HQRS. TRENCH MORTAR BATTERIES R.A.
41 DIVISION

Instructions regarding War Diaries and Intelligence Summaries are contained in F. S. Regs., Part II. and the Staff Manual respectively. Title Pages will be prepared in manuscript.

Vol 19

Place	Date	Hour	Summary of Events and Information	Remarks and references to Appendices
DICKEBUSCH N 1 b 2 5	SEPT. 1-2		HEADQUARTERS TRENCH MORTAR BATTERIES 41 DIVISION	
BOESCHEPE R 10 a 8 2	SEPT 2-13		MOVED INTO NEW BILLET for Rest.	
DICKEBOSCH N 3 b 2 4	SEPT 13-30		MOVED INTO NEW BILLET	

[signature] CAPT. R.F.A.
D.T.M.O., 41st Division

Instructions regarding War Diaries and Intelligence Summaries are contained in F. S. Regs., Part II, and the Staff Manual respectively. Title pages will be prepared in manuscript.

WAR DIARY ~~or~~ ~~INTELLIGENCE SUMMARY.~~

(*Erase heading not required.*)

OCTOBER 1917

V/41 TRENCH MORTAR BATTERY

Army Form C. 2118.

Place	Date	Hour	Summary of Events and Information	Remarks and references to Appendices
			This battery left the Ypres Sector on the 7th inst & took over the Newport Bains sector, relieving V/1, on the 14th. Firing consisted of retaliatory fire at the request of the Infantry until the 29th when it was relieved by V/9. Casualties nil.	
			On the 41st T.M.B proceeding to a new front V/41 HTMB was disbanded, the personnel being sent to reinforce field batteries & the D.A.C.	
			Capt J D Barin was attached to the 9th D. A 31/10/17	
			2/Lt ~~W G~~ W.M. Pratt was posted to X/41 T M B & 2/Lt F. W. Pope was posted to Z/41 T.M.B. 31/10/17	
			Frank W. Pope 2/Lt RFA V/41 HTMB	

D. D. & L., London, E.C. (A7883) Wt. W809/M1672 350,000 4/17 Sch. 52a Forms/C/2118/14

OCTOBER 1917

Army Form C. 2118.

Instructions regarding War Diaries and Intelligence Summaries are contained in F. S. Regs., Part II. and the Staff Manual respectively. Title pages will be prepared in manuscript.

WAR DIARY

~~or~~

~~INTELLIGENCE SUMMARY.~~ X/41 TRENCH MORTAR BATTERY

(Erase heading not required.)

Place	Date	Hour	Summary of Events and Information	Remarks and references to Appendices
			The battery left the Ypres sector on the 7th inst, but had not been in action there in this month. On the 14th the battery took over 3 2" guns in the Nieuport Bains sector & remained in action until the 29th when the 9th Divisional T M's took over. No firing was done except for retaliation.	
			No casualties occurred & no change in personnel.	

A W Pewtress
Lt. RFA.
OC X 41

D. D. & L., London, E.C.
(A7883) Wt. W803/M1672 350,000 4/17 Sch. 52a Forms/C/2118/14

Instructions regarding War Diaries and Intelligence Summaries are contained in F. S. Regs., Part II. and the Staff Manual respectively. Title pages will be prepared in manuscript.

WAR DIARY
or
~~INTELLIGENCE SUMMARY.~~
(Erase heading not required.)

OCTOBER 1917

Y/41 TRENCH MORTAR BATTERY

Army Form C. 2118.

Place	Date	Hour	Summary of Events and Information	Remarks and references to Appendices
			This battery left the Ypres sector on the 7th inst. On the 14th the battery took over 4 6" Newton Mortars in the Nieuport Bains sector until relieved by the 9th D.W. on the 29th inst. During this period firing in retaliation for hostile Trench Mortars was undertaken.	
			Casualties:-	
			N. 47166 Cpl J. Spencer wounded, but remained with Unit	
			N. 138621 Gnr F. Hill Wounded	
			N. 193716 " A. Williamson Wounded	
			2/Lt M.W.B. Ward was attached to the battery on the 31st inst	

A E Cundall
Lt R.F.A.
Y/41 T.M.B

D. D. & L., London, E.C.
(A7883) Wt. W803/M1672 350,000 4/17 Sch. 52a Forms/C/2118/14

OCTOBER 1917

Instructions regarding War Diaries and Intelligence Summaries are contained in F. S. Regs., Part II. and the Staff Manual respectively. Title pages will be prepared in manuscript.

WAR DIARY ~~or INTELLIGENCE SUMMARY.~~ Z/41 TRENCH MORTAR BATTERY

(*Erase heading not required.*)

Army Form C. 2118.

Place	Date	Hour	Summary of Events and Information	Remarks and references to Appendices
			This Battery left the Ypres sector on the 7th inst. On the 14th the battery went into action in the Nieuport Bains sector & assisted Y Battery in firing 4 6" Newton Mortars in retaliation for hostile Trench Mortars until relieved by the 9th Div on the 29th inst.	
			Casualties:—	
			Nil.	
			A. Fuller Lt R.F.A Z/41 T.M.B	

D. D. & L., London, E.C.
(A7883) Wt. W803/M1672 350,000 4/17 Sch. 52a Forms/C/2118/14

24

Instructions regarding War Diaries and Intelligence Summaries are contained in F. S. Regs., Part II. and the Staff Manual respectively. Title pages will be prepared in manuscript.

WAR DIARY
or
~~INTELLIGENCE SUMMARY.~~

(Erase heading not required.)

OCTOBER 1917

HEADQUARTERS TRENCH MORTAR BATTERIES 41 DIV

Army Form C. 2118.

Vol 20

Place	Date	Hour	Summary of Events and Information	Remarks and references to Appendices
DICKEBUSCH	OCT 1 – OCT 7		HEADQUARTERS TRENCH MORTAR BATTERIES 41 DIVISION	
DUNKIRK ST. POL.	OCT 7		MOVED INTO NEW BILLET FOR REST.	
COXYDE BAINS	OCT 12		MOVED INTO NEW BILLET.	
GHYVELDE	OCT 29		MOVED INTO NEW BILLET.	

G. Tilley CAPT. R.F.A.
D.T.M.O., 41st Division

D. D. & L., London, E.C.
(A7883) Wt. W803/M1672 350,000 4/17 Sch. 52a Forms/C/2118/14

www.ingramcontent.com/pod-product-compliance
Lightning Source LLC
Chambersburg PA
CBHW081553160426
43191CB00011B/1922

* 9 7 8 1 4 7 4 5 2 0 0 5 8 *